YOU ARE NOT YOUR LIMITS

YOU ARE NOT YOUR LIMITS

Javeno Mclean

LEAP

First published in the UK in 2025 by LEAP
An imprint of Bonnier Books UK
5th Floor, HYLO, 105 Bunhill Row,
London, EC1Y 8LZ

Copyright © Javeno Mclean, 2025

All rights reserved.

No part of this publication may be reproduced, stored or transmitted in any form or by any means, electronic, mechanical, photocopying or otherwise, without the prior written permission of the publisher.

The right of Javeno Mclean to be identified as Author of this work has been asserted by him in accordance with the Copyright, Designs and Patents Act, 1988.

A CIP catalogue record for this book is available from the British Library.

Hardback ISBN: 9781785122309

Also available as an ebook and an audiobook

1 3 5 7 9 10 8 6 4 2

Design and Typeset by Envy Design Ltd
Printed and bound in Great Britain by Clays Ltd, Elcograf S.p.A.

MIX
Paper | Supporting responsible forestry
FSC® C018072

Every reasonable effort has been made to trace copyright holders of material reproduced in this book, but if any have been inadvertently overlooked the publishers would be glad to hear from them.

The authorised representative in the EEA is
Bonnier Books UK (Ireland) Limited.
Registered office address: Floor 3, Block 3, Miesian Plaza,
Dublin 2, D02 Y754, Ireland
compliance@bonnierbooks.ie

www.bonnierbooks.co.uk

CONTENTS

Foreword by Lauren Steadman MBE — ix
Introduction by Ben Shephard — xiii
Prologue — 1
1. A DOOR OPENS — 9
2. AND THEN THERE WAS ONE — 25
3. THE OPTIONS ARE LIMITLESS — 53
4. IF YOU BUILD IT, THEY WILL COME — 79
5. IT TAKES A VILLAGE — 95
6. YOU ARE SEEN — 107
7. CHANNEL YOUR INNER DOG — 123
8. YOU ARE A LEADER — 139
9. LIFTING EACH OTHER UP — 157
10. ABSORBING THE PAIN AND BRINGING THE SUNSHINE — 179
11. WHAT'S NEXT? — 191

Acknowledgements — 205

*To anyone who has ever felt alone and not seen.
To anyone who needs hope and a reminder of how
unbelievable they are. This is for you.*

FOREWORD

There are some books that lift you. This is one of them.

From the very first page of *You Are Not Your Limits*, you can feel the pulse of something special – not just a story about a gym or even about fitness, but a story about a community that is built on love, respect, and an unshakable belief in the human spirit.

What Javeno McLean has created at J7 is far bigger than a health centre. It's a home for many, a safe haven to escape to, and a stage where people who have often been overlooked, underestimated, or counted out get to shine – not in spite of their challenges, but alongside them. The result is magical.

Whether you've come to this book as someone working in health, education, social care, or simply as a reader, you'll be introduced to some unforgettable people. Kiera, Josh, Brenda, DJ, Tallulah – these are not just clients or gym members, they are warriors, role models, superheroes in their own right.

YOU ARE NOT YOUR LIMITS

Each of their journeys is a lesson in resilience, humour, courage, and hope. Each story reminds us that behind every diagnosis or perceived 'limitation', there is a whole human being with power, passion, and purpose. Its ability not disability.

Javeno doesn't train people with a clipboard and stopwatch. He trains with his whole heart. His sessions aren't for aesthetics or the Instagrammable photos – they're about rediscovering joy, regaining confidence, reclaiming agency. And he does it all with a sense of fun that is as infectious as it is disarming.

What's perhaps most beautiful about this book is how clearly it shows that *true inclusivity isn't about ticking boxes – it's about seeing people*. Seeing them fully. Believing in them, even before they believe in themselves. And standing beside them, day after day, until they do.

In a world that so often feels divided, cynical, or obsessed with image, *You Are Not Your Limits* is a loud and joyful reminder of what matters. Kindness. Connection. Showing up. Celebrating small wins. Laughing hard. Helping someone stand – whether physically, emotionally, or spiritually – and letting them know they are not alone.

Javeno writes like he speaks: with warmth, honesty, and a wild, boundless energy. You'll hear his voice on every page — sometimes shouting encouragement, sometimes cracking jokes, sometimes breaking your heart with how deeply he cares. It's a rare and wonderful thing to come

FOREWORD

across a person so genuinely driven by purpose. And it's even more special to witness how that purpose radiates outward – into his gym, his community, and now, through this book, into the lives of readers everywhere.

This isn't just a memoir. It's a movement.

You might come away from this book inspired to work out. Or invited to reimagine what accessibility really looks like. Or to reach out to someone who's struggling. Whatever it stirs in you – trust it. Because *You Are Not Your Limits* is more than a title. It's a truth. One that Javeno and the incredible people he trains prove every single day.

Lauren Steadman MBE

INTRODUCTION

The world of social media can be a confusing, overwhelming place. Amongst the political grievances, the influencing life-stylers, the conspiracy theorists and the endless cat videos (I do love a good cat video), every now and again you come across something that will not only put a smile on your face, it will inspire you and renew your faith in human nature.

The day I discovered Javeno on Instagram was one of those occasions. For whatever reason, my algorithm on this particular day decided that I needed cheering up. I needed to see the best of what humans can be: selfless, larger than life, big, proud, patient, joyous, all within those bright orange walls.

Everything about that first glimpse of Javeno: his clients, his team, and his community was an assault on the senses – for all the right reasons. The aforementioned bright, uncompromising orange walls, the loud music, the even louder chat and merciless teasing, cajoling and encouragement. The people being pushed to excel, to flourish and thrive regardless of their mobility, medical history, or age. I'd never seen anything like it.

I devoured his videos. Each one rich in moments of laughter, physical endeavour, creativity, outdoing expectations and most powerfully of all, hope.

Whether you're watching Javeno training Keira who, post brain tumour, is dancing, lifting, laughing or being Bear Grylls in the woods. Or watching the amazing DJ, who has Down's syndrome, completing his first muscle up (this made me cry as I still can't do one, so I know how hard it is!). Or John who, post seven cardiac arrests, smashes through a stack of chairs named Gary Neville, followed by another bigger stack named Jaap Stam before finally scoring a goal by knocking a cone off a bench with a football. Or young Noah, who has autism, going on a safari walk around the gym and car park looking for wild animals, developing everything from his mobility, to flexibility strength and, crucially, confidence. Each and every one is magical.

I'm not the only one either. He has had millions of views across his various platforms as more of the world becomes aware of the movement he is creating, the community he is developing, the magic he is sharing. In a society that increasingly feels divided and isolating, Javeno is doing everything he can to fight that idea. He is the voice of community, bringing people together, sharing

INTRODUCTION

his passion to help everyone and anyone achieve far more than even they think they can, physically, mentally and emotionally.

Back in 2016 when I was hosting ITV's breakfast show *Good Morning Britain*, we launched a new campaign called 1 Million Minutes. It's a campaign about trying to combat loneliness. The idea being that viewers would donate time, not money, to causes and charities that would connect them with those who were feeling lonely.

As part of the campaign (which has had nearly one billion minutes donated to date) we have a series of awards honouring people doing extraordinary things to combat loneliness. In 2023, Javeno was the recipient of the Local Loneliness Hero award. This award aims to recognise an individual or group of any age who helps make a real difference to the community and to help people feel included, supported, involved and empowered to enjoy life within their community through volunteering. He epitomised what this award is all about.

It was wonderful to see him being recognised by not just those in his community, but also on a national platform too. He brought his energy, joy and irrepressibly enormous smile to London for the live television show and it was every bit as special to meet him in person as I knew it would be.

This wasn't the first and it certainly won't be the last award he wins. Of course, he isn't doing it for awards,

YOU ARE NOT YOUR LIMITS

he's doing it because that is just who he is. It's what drives him. It's what makes him Javeno.

Javeno's message reminds me of the idea that people may forget what you said or did, but won't forget how you made them feel. His superpower is that he makes people feel that whatever the challenge ahead of them may be, they can do it. That's his purpose, his energy, his expertise, his entire being. It's all about making everyone he comes into contact with, that trusts him with their physical wellbeing regardless of how delicate it may be or what their medical background is, to banish their doubts. He empowers individuals to disregard their concerns, forget their fears and when he asks them to try and do something seemingly impossible, to trust him and believe that they can, just as *he* believes they can.

I know you are going to love this book as much as I have. I really hope, like me, it leaves you with the reassurance that despite how it sometimes feels, life does have shining lights like Javeno . . . you just need to find them. And once you have, you trust them when they tell you that they believe in you and that you are not your limits, because that's the Javeno way.

Ben Shephard

PROLOGUE

One fateful night in 2015, I sat at my mum's kitchen table with a piece of paper and a biro, and I started writing. I had this vision of something that I desperately wanted – no, *needed* – to make happen, more than anything in the world. I knew it was simple, but it wouldn't be easy. It would be a big leap. I would have to quit my job, for a start, and get together a load of money to make it happen. But I had this intense, personal ambition that had started as a passing thought and was now burning fiercely inside me. And I wanted to make it real.

My dream was to start a health and fitness centre that would be a place where good energy could flow. I lived in Manchester: a city diverse in its people, architecture and history. A few miles north of the centre is an area called Blackley, which is faced with a lot of socio-economic challenges as well as the changes brought on by regeneration. I knew this place could become the beating heart of the community.

I envisioned a place where anybody and everybody could come and train together: young, old, Black, White, Asian, professional athletes, complete beginners. A safe space where disabled and disadvantaged individuals could train and feel empowered. Any human being would be welcome there: anybody at all. This place would be all on one floor. It would only have one door to come in and go out, so everybody could interact and mingle. It would be a space where elderly people could be jamming to Elvis while a young man tried powerlifting for the first time and a person in a wheelchair nailed their pull-ups. And it would be filled with positivity and a ridiculous amount of contagious love.

Well, that should be easy enough, right . . . ?

Don't get me wrong – I loved the job I had. I'd spent over a decade working for Manchester City Council, setting up and running almost any kind of exercise class and training you can imagine. My mission was to *get Manchester active*. The job felt special and it had taught me a lot. It's sometimes said that you are a product of your community. I learned that every person in a group, who takes part in something, can influence another person there. That a community is created by those who stand up and care and give of themselves. If a person has a message, and a passion, and shouts loud, they can

PROLOGUE

influence a whole community. I knew I had a passion for and a message about exercise and fitness, and a voice loud enough to get it across. So, why wasn't my current job enough? The answer was simple. It was a great vision – *but it wasn't mine*. I wanted to do more.

At this point, all I had was an idea. A load of scrawl on a piece of paper. But I started saving some money from my salary each month while I carried on working for the council, squirrelling away a bit here and a bit there. It made me feel like I was at least working towards my goal, even if I didn't know how long it would take to achieve it.

I was dreaming a big dream. And, as I sat there at the table that evening, I could never have imagined where it would lead me – or, specifically, the incredible, inspiring people I would meet, or the magic I would one day see happening in front of my eyes.

This book is partly the story of how it all came about, and what it's taught me about love, community and passion. But it's mostly about the people who came through the door, with their positivity, strength and determination not to accept any limits placed on them, no matter what physical challenges they might be facing. It's those people who have made my little health centre the magical place it is today. They also, through the power of social media, inspire people around the world every day.

While my team and I will always be grateful for the social media growth we have seen over the last few years, it will never be our priority. It's incredible to see the level of support that floods in from around the world for our superstars, but nothing will ever come before the work we're doing to improve their health.

Every day, I get to see just how unbreakable the human spirit is. I have never met a bunch of individuals who are more disciplined or open to positivity than the people who walk through the doors of our health centre. There's only so much a two-minute viral clip can show you, so we knew it was time to do something bigger.

What you see online is just the tip of the iceberg. A lot of people might question if the clips are truthful reflections of how we work, day in, day out. So, this book will give you a behind-the-scenes look at how the health centre really came into being. More importantly, it contains the fuller stories of the inspirational superstars I've had the privilege of working with, told from their own perspectives. These days, it's so easy to feel disillusioned with the world or to lose sight of what matters. Happiness, acceptance, peace . . . those are the things we should be chasing. As the stories here will show, this really is the stuff that glues us together as humans.

There are too many incredible stories to fit into one book, but – with great difficulty – I have picked a few individuals' journeys to share in the chapters that follow.

You'll meet Kiera, a warrior who refuses to give up; Josh, who taught me the real power in strength; Paul, who

PROLOGUE

proves it's never too late to reinvent yourself; Brenda, a role model for really living your life to the fullest; DJ, a beacon of positivity and joy; Aimee, a survivor with a remarkable mindset; Noah, a masterclass in having a strong work ethic; Fran, a leading inspirational figure; and Tallulah, a firm believer that the sky is the only limit.

When I first met Kiera, she said, 'I'm here because I'm going to give it a go, because I want to get better, but I don't believe I will.' It broke my heart to see someone so openly defeated. Nothing fuels me more than my drive to show people that no matter what has happened to them, their life is not over. I will go to great lengths to show someone that I won't give up on them. Whether it's training outside in the mud, crawling about on the floor of the health centre, getting pied in the face or hit by water balloons, I will do whatever is needed to make our training sessions fun and motivational.

I realised quickly that we needed to be different. We couldn't just offer eight-week training programmes then send people off, wishing them all the best. We had to be about more than counting reps and constantly asking, 'You ready?' We needed to take a completely different approach to health.

Inclusivity is a simple but very important word. To me, it means thinking about other people. It's understanding that something may not affect me, but what about you? It's more than putting up a disabled toilet sign, adding handrails to a facility, or ticking off adaptations on a checklist. It means *seeing* people. Real inclusivity is a mindset. It's about creating an environment where people feel safe to come on their worst days as well as their best days, where they can make mistakes and grow, while being free of judgement.

When we come together in spaces where *anyone* can feel like they belong, we all get the power to do amazing things. We find new ways of motivating and inspiring each other, and we find out that we are capable of so much more than we ever thought.

I've seen first-hand that you can be going through the worst situation, you can have so much taken away from you, but by coming together with others, and expressing genuine care, you draw on an endless well of strength. I've met a lot of people who were born able-bodied but have had something happen to them which changed their life overnight. I hope the stories in this book show why it's so important to be someone's ladder, or to simply be in their corner, because – despite our differences – there are times when we all need a helping hand. It's one of the best ways we can make each other feel valued, to show up and say, 'I see you. You're not alone. Let's do this together.'

This book is not just for people who may be disabled, or people who may be carers: this book is for everyone. We all experience highs and lows in life. We all have to learn the power of resilience, discipline and healing. And

PROLOGUE

it's easy to forget just how powerful we are, as humans. That's what I hope these stories will show you. We are all so much stronger than we think.

These have been strange times for many of us, with a lot of negative stuff going on, but I truly believe that this new way of seeing the world is what's needed at the moment. When we help somebody from the purest part of our soul, and accept help when we need it, that's when we don't just survive, but start to thrive. That's when we really understand that we are not our limits.

1.
A DOOR OPENS

KIERA:

I had a brain tumour in 2020, when I was 19. I was in college, studying hair and makeup. Then Covid came along so we were all working remotely. I was focusing on the main bit of work for my exam on the day I got diagnosed with the tumour. The doctors warned me there was a 70 per cent chance that it was cancerous.

That April, I had a 15-hour brain operation. The surgeons removed the tumour. After the operation, I could hardly move. I stayed in hospital, they gave me proton radiation and I started getting better. I had mobility issues, but I was on the mend. But in the September, I had to start eight months of chemotherapy.

It was awful. The proton radiation had only

targeted my brain, but the chemo went into my whole body via a port-a-cath in my chest. They didn't put it in my hand because I was so young that they didn't want to ruin it. I lost so much weight and felt sick all the time. I couldn't do anything.

My whole body collapsed. I felt like a skittle in a ten-pin bowling alley. I'd been knocked down and I was getting back up again, slowly. But then I was sent crashing down again, harder and worse than I'd ever been. I couldn't have felt any lower.

The chemo finished in April 2021 and it left me badly disabled. I could hardly stand, let alone walk, and I had a speech impairment. At the same time, my nan, who I was close to, died. I'm not going to lie: I wanted to do the same. All I could think was: Why? Why me? *I didn't want to go on. I didn't see the point. I was suicidal.*

I felt like my life was over. Nothing seemed worthwhile. And then a friend sent me a few of Javeno's J7 videos. She said, 'I think he'd be good for you.' And I watched them and thought, No! No way! I remember saying to my mum, 'I don't think we'll get on! We'll clash! Because he is so loud, and I hate loudness and loud people!'

But they persuaded me to message him. Javeno replied, and I went to see him. And my life changed again.

A DOOR OPENS

I was right, he is dead loud, but in a good way. A way that inspires me. And I didn't hate him. I absolutely loved him.

In July 2023, something quite miraculous happened at the little gym that I run in Blackley, North Manchester, otherwise known as J7. If I'm being honest, I like to think that miracles happen there all the time. Like I said, it's a magical place. But this was really, really special.

One of the many brave people I've had the privilege of working with, since I made my health centre dream a reality in 2017, is Kiera. Kiera is a beautiful young woman who used to go out partying and doing normal teenage things around Manchester. But then she had a brain tumour, and the consequent chemotherapy damaged all her nerves. In fact, it impacted them so badly that Kiera has had to learn how to walk again.

That is a lot for any human being to cope with, so it is lucky that Kiera is one of the most determined and resilient young people I've ever met. She and I have been through a lot together and her sheer willpower never fails to impress me. But what she did one summer day, back in 2023, was out of this world . . .

In fact, it was so brilliant that I filmed a one-minute video of her and put it on Instagram and TikTok. It starts with Kiera arriving at the gym. First, she gets out of the front passenger seat of the car without any help.

YOU ARE NOT YOUR LIMITS

She puts one hand on top of the door and one on the frame before pulling herself up. I'm encouraging her: 'Go on, K-Boogie!'

Kiera steadies herself, gets her balance and walks across the pavement to J7. I'm next to her, but I don't need to support her. She puts her hand on the door . . . and opens it.

It may not sound like much on paper but, believe me, for someone who's been through what Kiera has, it's monumental. The concentration on her face was intense.

Being Kiera, she wanted to do it all at record speed.

'Stop! Balance! Get your chin up!' I tell her as we go into the gym. She steadies herself and walks again. 'She's legging it! She's leggy with it, bro!' I yell as she continues walking, all the way to a chair that I'd got ready for her. And, still totally under her own steam, she sits down.

The video went viral. I mean, *proper* viral. The gym's social media following had already gone through the roof by that point, much to my initial surprise, but huge gratitude. The internet is a great way to show the world what the warriors within our walls are achieving. But Kiera's video touched people's hearts all round the world. At the time of writing, it has been viewed on TikTok *more than 23 million times.*

For a girl who couldn't walk *at all* a few months earlier, this was unbelievable. For me, it's up there with Keely Hodgkinson winning an Olympic gold medal for Team

A DOOR OPENS

GB. Not only did 23 million people watch Kiera do it on our socials, but 55,000 of them left her messages telling her she was ace. I hope she read every one of them. She deserves to.

Kiera is just one of the brilliant people I train in my little gym right near where I grew up and still live in Manchester. I train many talented souls – and I do it by putting the emphasis on their potential, not their disabilities. Because I look beyond their disabilities and conditions. I see *them*.

Because, you know what? Forget 'disabled'! The important word is *people*. As I say to everybody who comes into my gym, I don't care about what they can't do. That's not important to me. I care about what they *can* do. They may have physical limitations but they are so, so much more than that.

I tell them: *you are not your limits.*

We live in a strange world nowadays, and through social media, my little gym has somehow achieved fame around the world. More than half a million people follow it on Instagram and over a million on TikTok. I have to pinch myself sometimes: *I mean, it's ridiculous, right?* But if I'm honest, I really don't care about those numbers.

Because it's not about me. It's not even about J7. What it *is* about, is the millions of people all over the world, watching amazing young people, like Kiera – and Aimee and Josh and Francesca (who you'll meet later) and all the others – and sending them online words of love and encouragement. That encouragement means more to the guys I train than you can possibly imagine. It makes them feel like *superstars*: role models who can harness their ability to inspire people in the same situation as them. I feel so grateful to be part of their journey, to be able to help them access their own ability to shine and grow.

*

One part of my mission was to redefine what a gym is. You know what? I hate the word 'gym'. It scares and intimidates a lot of people. And I can see why.

Gyms can be really lonely places. I'm a gym person, and I must have trained in every bloody gym in Manchester. Yet even *I* have been in gyms where I've felt lonely and intimidated. And I'm a big, strapping, confident bloke. So, how must some other people feel?

There are some gyms where groups of people look at you just because you're different. Well, think how much worse that can be for people who lack confidence and don't know about gyms. Older people, for example. When they hear the word 'gym', they shake their heads because they picture musclebound machines. They say, 'Oh, no, no, no, not for me!' before they've even set foot in one. And I don't blame them. This is another reason why I prefer to label myself an 'exercise specialist' rather than a 'personal trainer'. I think some people have a fixed image in their heads of what a personal trainer is or should be,

A DOOR OPENS

but I wanted people to visit our health centre and know that they could start with a clean slate, regardless of where they were in their fitness journey.

I wanted to change how people see fitness so that an older person could go to the gym and enjoy it. One of my proudest achievements is that I have elderly or disabled clients who will happily say, 'I'm going to the gym on Friday!' They're excited about it, because the experience isn't frightening. It's fun.

That's why I decided not to call my place, J7, a gym. On the front, it says 'J7 Health Centre'. That won't scare *anybody* off. And, even if you want to call it a gym, which you can if you like, it's a *welcoming* gym. A place to feel safe and accepted, not intimidated and lonely. The main thing I want to do in my sessions is make sure the person is having fun. I just want people to enjoy life. It's about making someone feel seen and valued through exercise.

When I look back now – with the benefit of hindsight – I can tell you the exact moment when I knew what I was going to do with my life. I can't tell you *why* I did what I did. I can't tell you what made me do it. But I *can* tell you exactly what happened.

I was 16 years old, so it would have been 2001. I was running a sports coaching session for Manchester City Council. I'd always been mad for sport, ever since I was tiny, so naturally I took training classes to become a coach. The council used to give me children's sessions to coach

'It's about making someone feel seen and valued through exercise.'

A DOOR OPENS

in the school breaks. We'd do week-long multi-sports camps in local parks during half-terms, the Easter break and the six-week summer holidays. They were fantastic. It was a nice bit of money in my teenage pocket but, more than that, I just loved teaching kids to play sport – to *enjoy* sport.

Cricket was my first love, and this particular day I was doing a cricket session for twelve young lads at a park in Cheetham Hill. It was a roasting hot day, the ice cream vans were out and my boys were getting right into our game. Despite all the activity, I couldn't take my eyes off something that was happening on the other side of the park.

I saw a family playing cricket together – about eight of them, all different ages, buzzing and running around. They were dead loud and really enjoying themselves. But it wasn't their cricket match that had grabbed my attention. No. I was watching a guy who was watching them.

To the side of their game but obviously part of their group was a man in a wheelchair. He was probably in his fifties. He was watching his family intently while they played cricket. Every time someone ran in to bowl, or a batsman clouted the ball hard, his face would react. He was following every ball. His fingers were twitching as if he was playing the shots. And I realised: *He wants in! The guy wants in!*

This man was in a wheelchair but he wanted to play

cricket so much that it hurt. I could *feel* it, even fifty yards away across a busy Manchester park. All my life, I have hated injustice, and it seemed so unfair for him to be sat there. It bugged me.

It was none of my business, really. It was a family who were out, having fun, and I was a skinny 16-year-old kid who didn't even know them. I had no right to do anything and yet, even so, I *knew*, in my heart, that I had to do something. I instructed the kids I was coaching to carry on without me for a minute and I marched across the park.

I stood by the guy in the wheelchair. His family stopped playing and looked at me. And I asked them a question: 'Excuse me, who is this man?'

'He's my dad,' one of them answered.

'My uncle,' another one said.

'My grandad,' a little kid piped up.

'Well, how dare you leave him out?' I asked them. 'How dare you not get him involved? It's a beautiful day and you lot are having the best time in the world. How dare you miss him out and leave him sitting in the shade, like he's a plant?'

There was silence as they absorbed my words. Looking back, I'm surprised they didn't punch me in the face. They probably should have done. I had no right to speak to them like that, but I was just full of emotion and only 16. Nobody said anything, though. They seemed a bit lost for words. And so I took control.

A DOOR OPENS

'Right, here's what we're going to do!' I said. 'We're *all* going to play cricket!' I asked the guy in the wheelchair his name. 'Ishmael,' he replied. With his permission, I pushed him to the cricket pitch his family were playing on and called the kids from my coaching session over to join us. Everybody gathered round me.

I put Ishmael in front of the wicket and handed him the cricket bat. 'Big man, can you swing it?' I asked him. He waved the bat in the air and beamed.

'OK,' I said to the others. 'You're all going to take it in turns to bowl to Ishmael. If he hits the ball, nothing happens. If he misses it, you've all got to do one press-up. Got it?'

Everyone nodded. And for the next hour and a half, we had a great game of cricket. Ishmael was the only guy who batted. And you have never seen a man enjoy himself so much! Every time he hit the ball, his face glowed. I could see his grin, his aura, his energy, his *existence,* growing before my eyes. Man, I've got to tell you, it was amazing!

Ishmael was lit up from inside. When the game finished, his wife came over and hugged me. She was only a tiny lady and she didn't speak a word of English, but she hugged me tight for ages and she didn't let go. You could see what it meant to her.

And to Ishmael, who spoke in broken English. He hadn't been born disabled, he told me. He'd had a bad accident, 12 years earlier, which had left him in a wheelchair.

YOU ARE NOT YOUR LIMITS

And then Ishmael said something I'll never forget: 'This is the first time that I have felt alive in 12 years.'

It was such a powerful moment. I still find it hard to articulate exactly why I went over to that family who had nothing to do with me, but I'm so glad I did. Because that moment led me to do what I have done for the rest of my life so far.

It made me realise that what I really love is helping people and making them smile. It's about training disabled people – and simply seeing them as individuals. It means not seeing the wheelchair but the *person* in it. Seeing people like *Ishmael*.

You know what? I'm a very lucky man. A chance encounter, in a park in Cheetham Hill in Manchester one summer afternoon, showed me my calling and exactly what I wanted to do with my life. And I'm so glad it did. Because I wouldn't change it for the world. Without that random event, I might not have met people like Josh and Kiera, and all the others you're going to meet, who inspire me every day.

*

The majority of my J7 superstars were born disabled. They have been wheelchair-bound or lived with disabilities for their entire lives. It's what they're used to. They have bad days like all of us, of course, when they feel frustrated or heartbroken, but that's generally not caused by their

A DOOR OPENS

disability. More often than not, it's due to being treated horribly by society, or trying to navigate a world that's not been set up with enough consideration for them.

Some of my other clients are people who were born able-bodied, but then had something catastrophic happen to them. Naturally, their emotional journey can be very different, and their bad days are sometimes more closely linked to their disability. They have had so much change to come to terms with, and they sometimes have to deal with a lot of trauma from when they first got ill or got injured.

Kiera belongs to the second group. When she had her brain tumour, and the chemotherapy messed up her nervous system so badly, she had to learn to walk again, and it was a lot for her to cope with. It would be a lot for *any* human being to cope with. The first time I met her, when she came into J7, all I could see was somebody who really wanted to be OK. She had been through this horrible ordeal – the chemo had damaged her nerves and her self-confidence was quite low. But she was desperate to show the world, *I'm OK. I'm still an independent, strong woman.*

The vibe I got off Kiera was frustration. But you know what? I love frustration! I love it when I see people who are frustrated, because I think frustration is a blessing. As John Lydon once sang, 'Anger is an energy'. Frustration can be a blessing that helps you turn pain into purpose and achievement.

YOU ARE NOT YOUR LIMITS

The other thing I very quickly discovered is that Kiera is incredibly determined. It humbles me right down to my socks. Every step that she takes, every wobble, there is an underlying fear because she could easily fall and hurt herself. But she has the strength to get through that. To get past it. To give it a go. She really is one of the most driven and extraordinary young people I've ever met. It is an honour and a privilege to know her and to train her.

Kiera's got the ability to bounce back very quickly. If she does fall, or has a wobble, she sits down and takes a breather. She has a word with herself. She will give it everything. I'm her cheerleader. I'm right there with her and I feel so proud every time she accomplishes something. When I see Kiera bend down and pick up a weight, after all she's been through, it's like seeing an Olympic athlete winning a gold medal. The effort and dedication she puts in is massive. When you look at how far she has come and what she has done to get there, it's easy to see that these are huge, huge achievements.

It's difficult to put into words just how much she has accomplished. I got her doing a squat with an 11kg bar on her back. She was scared and not sure she could do it, but I reassured her and she took a deep breath before giving it a go. She bent those knees, went down, then straightened up again – marvellous! Then, to prove it wasn't a one-off, she did it twice more.

Her balance and co-ordination were impacted by the

A DOOR OPENS

chemo but, one brilliant day, I got her jumping over a skipping rope. I could tell that Kiera could hardly believe that she had done it afterwards. She felt the same when she stood and threw a basketball through a hoop. This was a woman who once feared she'd never walk again!

With a lot of the people I train, I try to incorporate elements into the session that will help with their everyday lives. For instance, I've re-taught Kiera some practical stuff, such as hoovering. I gave her a vacuum cleaner and asked her to hoover up the talcum powder I kept dropping on the floor. I'd spill it further and further away from her, to make her move to reach it: 'Look, K, you missed a bit!'

'You knobhead!' she laughed – and hoovered up every last bit.

I'm always learning as a trainer and I've learned a lot from Kiera. Together we've figured out how to use frustration to our advantage. We've found we can work with her emotions, and her pain, to create something positive and powerful. It's been an emotional process and it's been very rewarding, for both of us.

KIERA:

Javeno doesn't think going to the gym just means getting big muscles. He does stuff with me that means something. Stuff I can take away from the session. He re-teaches me things that I used to do easily as an able-bodied person. It can be as simple as putting washing into a basket. Or vacuuming. Or opening a fridge. Or picking up a cup of tea.

Every time we train, we do something new. The hardest thing Javeno has made me do recently was to step up onto boxes. When I managed it, he'd challenge me by putting another box on top and encourage me to do it again. By the end, I felt like I was stepping onto a tower! It would be easy for an able person but for me it was so, so hard.

Javeno has got so much energy, and that's exactly what I need because I don't want to feel all mopey. If I see him in the morning, it puts me in a good mood for the rest of the day. At the start of 2024, Javeno said to me, 'Right, Kiera. This year, we're going to go harder, and make things harder, and you're going to work harder!' And I admit, I thought, uh-oh! But hearing it was very motivational. Because he knows how hard to push me. And I feel myself getting stronger.

2.
AND THEN THERE WAS ONE

JOSH:

I was born with cerebral palsy and I've been in a wheelchair for my entire life. It's all I've ever known. I can't walk, but I'm able to crawl and move around on my hands and knees quite a bit – as anyone who's seen my videos in Javeno's gym will know!

Despite being in a wheelchair, I went to a mainstream school as a kid. It was tough at times, of course, but I was very much into the arts. I loved English and drama because I'd wanted to be a writer or an actor ever since I was a tiny kid. I'd always be writing my own scripts and I got involved in all the school plays.

YOU ARE NOT YOUR LIMITS

I still write now. I met a guy on Zoom called Scott Cartwright who writes plays and stage musicals. We decided to collaborate as Cartwright and Coy (my surname is Coy). We've co-written a stage musical adaptation of Pinocchio: *not the Disney version that everyone knows, but an adaptation of the original book. We hope to stage it one day.*

When my aunty told me about Javeno and showed me his sessions online, I wasn't sure at first about meeting him. It was a totally new thing for me and I suppose I was a bit scared. But then it turned out that J7 is literally five minutes away from where I live, so I thought: OK, let's give it a go. I thought it might be a good way to get fit.

My dad and my carer took me down the first time. And I'm so glad I went. Javeno was just totally genuine. One of the first things he ever said to me was: 'I don't care about what you can't do. I only care about what you can do.'

And that phrase has stuck with me ever since.

I had my first proper training session with Javeno a week after I met him. It was fairly easy at first, just to test the water: a bit of weightlifting and a little bit of boxing. And then he told me he was going to lift me out of my chair. I love being out of my chair. And I'm out of it a lot of the time at J7! I like it because it gives my body a full workout and I can get the most out of

AND THEN THERE WAS ONE

a session. But that's not the main reason. The main reason is that, when I'm out, I don't feel restrained.

When Javeno got me out of my chair and bouncing on a trampoline, that was very taxing because I had to hold on to the ropes to keep myself standing up. It was a lot of work for my upper body and lower body. But that's what Javeno's like. He pushes me hard but never too far. He goes as far as I'm willing to go.

When I'm out of my chair, he gets me crawling on the floor a lot. It's normally themed around animals. He'll lift me out, put me down on the mats, and say, 'Right, Josh! You're a donkey!' Or, 'You're an alligator!' I've been compared to all sorts of animals now. I guess he knows I like acting and drama!

I love that he does that. I mean, I'm enjoying the session anyway, but then Javeno comes out with all these crazy ideas and it makes it even more fun. What I like about him is that we never do the same thing twice. It's always something new, something fresh. And some sessions are easier than others.

Javeno challenges me a lot but I invite the challenge. Nine times out of ten, I will feel like I can do it. I've had moments when I feel that I can't, but I always give 110 per cent and, if I don't get it right on the first try, I give it another go. I persevere. I think, I want to see this through! And it works out in the end.

The sessions are never a chore. They're always

fun and engaging. Javeno goes further and further every time. Like the time he made me run around the car park. That was one of the hardest things I've ever done in my life. Mind you, Javeno always works me hard! That run was especially tough. But that's the thing about Javeno – he wouldn't push me to do something if he didn't know I was capable of doing it and that I wanted to do it.

After a session with Javeno, I always feel invigorated ... and exhausted! Most of all, I feel a real sense of pride that I was able to pull off whatever Javeno or his team asked me to do. I know for a fact that the training is just as important for my mental health as it is for my physical health. Getting the chance to do it is a blessing.

Javeno and I get each other. That's what I love about him and his team. They don't treat you as if you're just part of the job. They don't treat anyone like that. You feel you have a real friendship with them. The most important thing is that you feel as if you're part of a massive family.

I still have down, depressed days. Life isn't easy. I don't often get upset about my actual disability, but I've had a hard time over the last few years. I lost my mum, due to her own health complications. Even though she's not here anymore, Javeno has been a massive, important reason for me to keep smiling.

AND THEN THERE WAS ONE

Mind you, you should hear the things he calls me! He swears like a sailor . . .

I opened J7 in June 2017. I suppose it was what you'd call a soft launch. I didn't make a song and dance about it or have any kind of opening party. I didn't feel like I had anything to celebrate because I hadn't actually achieved anything yet. That was all in the future. We were only just getting started.

It had taken me a long time to find the venue. In my head, I knew exactly the sort of space I was looking for but so many places I saw didn't fit the bill. Some spaces were too big or too small. Others weren't in a great location, or just didn't feel right. I didn't want anything too big. It would have cost too much and, in any case, my vision was a compact, intimate space where everyone had room to train but we were all mixed in together. It also had to be near where I lived, in Blackley or Crumpsall. It had to be in the community. I didn't want a snazzy venue in Manchester city centre (not that I could have afforded it anyway!).

I've lived in the area for over 30 years, since I was five. When my family first arrived from Jamaica we lived in Didsbury, but soon moved to Crumpsall, in the north of the city. Crumpsall is next to Blackley, near where I live now. I love these communities – they're tight-knit and friendly. Though these parts of Manchester are often referred to as 'underprivileged'. The people are typical Mancs: quick to

'The most important thing is that you feel as if you're part of a massive family.'

AND THEN THERE WAS ONE

say hello and ask, 'You alright, our kid?' and equally quick to slap you down if you're out of line. I love that! If you ask me, it's how people should be.

That straightforward friendliness has had a big impact on me. I think that's what gave me the courage to go up and introduce myself to Ishmael and his family that day. I went to a primary school that was totally multicultural so I was never scared or wary of people who looked different from me. I appreciated them and wanted to know all about them.

At school, I made friends with Pakistani kids, and Polish kids, and bombarded them with questions: 'What food do you eat at home? What music do you listen to?' I didn't mean to be nosy, I just loved learning about different cultures and ways of living. I'd go home at night with my head spinning: 'Oh my God, there's so much out there in the world to find out about!'

So that was where the gym had to be. However, it wasn't easy finding the right space. When I *did* see a place I liked, I'd find that it had just gone, or someone else would come in and take it at the last minute. *Damn!* This went on for six months. All I could do was keep my eyes open, scour the property ads and go to see any local units that became available as quickly as possible.

And then I found it.

I looked at a unit tucked in the back of a little local parade of shops on Old Market Street in Blackley. The location was perfect. I got shown around the space and had a great feeling about it. It was still available. *OK, this is it!*

Deep breath. *Let's do this!* I signed the lease.

Once I had the space for J7, and I'd left my job, I set about setting the place up and sorting out the décor. And the first thing I did was to think very hard about colour. Colours are very important to me. They can tell a story, and they bring out feelings and emotions. Every colour has a different effect on people. I don't know if there's actual science behind it, but I believe in colours and I think they matter. So, I did a little bit of research into what they all signify.

For me, blue is a cold colour. Red is love, sure, but it's also an angry colour. Or you have purple, or lavender, which are kind of relaxing colours. That's why you often see them when you go to a spa. Well, I wanted J7 to be a welcoming place, but not *too* relaxing – there was work to be done there!

I'm a happy person and I wanted the health centre to reflect that feeling, so I started thinking about happy colours. For me, the main ones are yellow and orange. Yellow is happy because it's like sunshine, but sunshine is there, and then it's gone. It can be temporary and short-lived (especially in Manchester!). So, I decided to go with orange.

I painted the walls myself. It was a labour of love. There was no way I'd have brought in anyone else to do

AND THEN THERE WAS ONE

it. My brother helped me put all the mirrors up. The only thing I had to hire workmen for was to make the 'J7' signs and put them up. Everything else, I did with my own two hands. I wanted to make sure the centre was brought to life exactly as I'd imagined it.

If you're wondering about the name, well, the 'J' bit is easy as it's obviously short for Javeno, and what some of my friends and family call me (when they aren't calling me Toby! I'll explain about that later. Remind me). The '7' has more of a story to it. Basically, it's a number that seems to have followed me throughout my life.

When I was playing basketball at school, each kid had the same number every game. Mine was seven. When I played cricket, I always seemed to be number seven on the team roster, no matter which team I played for. My wife Laura's birthday is 7 December. Mason, my lad, was born on 7 January. I don't know if I believe in lucky numbers, as such, but seven has turned up in my life over the years in so many different ways. So why not keep it going? It made total sense to me to call the place J7. It just felt right.

There's a famous quote from an old American movie called *Field of Dreams*: 'If you build it, they will come.' The film is about a farmer, played by Kevin Costner, who builds a baseball stadium in one of his cornfields, powered by the blind faith that when it exists, people will flock to it. And that quote pretty much sums up my mentality when I first started trying to get my gym together.

YOU ARE NOT YOUR LIMITS

I'd decided to get nearly all free weights. If you go to a gym nowadays, whether it's a posh place like David Lloyd or the local council leisure centre, you'll see it's mostly made up of machines. And, sure, that stuff is OK, if that's your thing. But, to be honest, machines aren't always the most inclusive form of equipment. You can make some great progress using machines, but I'm all for people being able to rely on the strength of their own bodies. Mainly because it's one of the best ways for them to see exactly who they are and what they're capable of.

I also think fitness has been over-complicated. It doesn't have to be fancy and expensive. There are some people who are so bling that they'd probably like a set of gold dumbbells with diamonds cut in them, but, really, what's the point? I think this type of gym aesthetic, especially what we see online, can deter a lot of people from going to the gym or make them feel it's not a place they belong.

Fitness isn't about that. If you're playing football, it makes no difference if you're wearing £300 Predators boots or £7 Basics. Expensive equipment doesn't guarantee success. I knew I didn't need tons of pricey gym equipment. The trick is giving people magical moments and memorable experiences.

I'd actually started buying the equipment before I even had a venue. I'd be out and about, in a Fitness Superstore or Strength Shop, and buy two kettlebells, or a couple of gym balls. Or I'd pick up five exercise mats. I had a rough

AND THEN THERE WAS ONE

list of the things I wanted and I'd get them a few at a time.

I didn't tell anyone what I was doing back then. I knew if somebody asked me, 'Bro, why have you bought five mats?' and I told them, 'Because I'm going to open my own fitness centre!' they'd just give me a funny look: *yeah, right!* So, I kept quiet, carried on piling the stuff up and stashing it in my shed in the garden. I just kept plodding away in the direction of my dream and kept the faith that I could make the space I imagined a reality.

The start of the process was both exciting and daunting. I'd never run my own business before. I had loads of things to think about and work out, but I knew exactly what sort of place I wanted it to be.

*

For the first couple of years, I totally threw myself into the place. I mean, totally. I only took two days off in the first two years. I was there every day, from dawn till dusk. I took every single class myself. There were no breaks and definitely no holidays. I remember, one time, Laura and I got invited to a wedding in Cyprus. I told her, 'There's no way I can take the time off.' She ended up going on her own.

I was training mostly able-bodied people. Although I knew, from my past experiences working for the council, that I was good at training disabled people and I loved doing it. From day one at J7 the plan was always to give a home to disabled and disadvantaged people. And I wanted it to grow organically. I didn't even get flyers done because I wanted news to spread through word of mouth.

J7 was all about inclusivity. It was for everybody in the community, equally. And when I say community, I mean male, female, young, old, Black, White, tall, short, Asian, Muslim, Jewish. Everybody. That obviously, *obviously* included disabled people.

In the past, I had done a course about training people with disabilities. It was good for learning some practical, biomechanical things about stuff like blood pressure and heart rate. But the way it was delivered left a lot to be desired. I sat through a few days of dreary lectures with no energy, no presence, no what the French call *je ne sais quoi*. I remember thinking, *if any disabled people had to listen to this, they'd be bored silly.* I knew that when I trained disabled people, I'd take the knowledge but deliver it differently.

And sure enough, after J7 had been open for two years or so, disabled people in the community and those who were suffering from or recovering from life-changing conditions like cancer began making a beeline for the place. It happened slowly at first, and then very, very quickly. I loved working with people who had these challenges, and I guess the word about that quickly spread. Like all the best things, it happened entirely naturally and of its own accord, just as I'd hoped. I didn't make

AND THEN THERE WAS ONE

it happen: *it happened to me*, and to J7. I could not be happier that it did.

I hadn't seen this shift coming, but it was a fantastic development. It altered everything. The paying members kept the finances of the gym ticking over, and I trained my disabled clients for nothing. And that is what I have carried on doing ever since.

When a lot of disabled people started turning up at J7, I had a little process that I'd do with them. They'd often come in for a quick look around, in their wheelchairs or on their frames or crutches, with their parents or their carers. They'd normally be dead nervous. I'd go over, introduce myself, have a little chat, and then I'd ask: 'What are you doing now? Right now?'

'Oh, er, nothing,' they'd usually answer.

'OK!' I'd say. 'Let's go!'

I'd do a few things with them, there and then. I'd tell them, 'Try to touch the sky. Good! Now, try to touch the walls.' This was just to see what their flexibility and mobility were like. Then I'd hand them some dumbbells. 'Right,' I'd say. 'Give me ten bicep curls.'

They'd be wary at first. I'd see it in their faces. But, within five minutes, I'd see those guys thinking, *wow!* Because they'd be getting the message I was trying to give them: you are welcome here. This is a good environment for you. We're not going to slam the door in your face. We can do a lot of great things here – and we can have fun.

YOU ARE NOT YOUR LIMITS

I think a lot of people move through life and are made to feel like they can't be who they truly are. I feel so lucky that I get to be myself through my work, although it took a little while for me to figure myself out. I just want others to feel empowered enough to share in that feeling.

*

One day, I started training a woman in her sixties. She was very glamorous and confident, in a black wig and film-star dark glasses. She told me that, growing up, she was obsessed with Audrey Hepburn. And I thought, *who the hell is Audrey Hepburn?* After she left, I had to Google her.

I put the lady through a workout and, at the end of it, she told me that she had just had breast cancer. She'd been through chemotherapy (hence the wig) and had just had the all-clear and was getting moving again. And, when she told me, I wasn't shocked. I was impressed. I just saw a beautiful woman, willing to work to get herself well again.

She came in again, a couple of weeks later. I was halfway through a session with somebody else, so I said, 'Oi, you! Get over here! Come and join in!' I complimented her on how cool her wig looked and we cracked on. I could tell that she enjoyed the class . . . but then I didn't see her again for a few weeks.

I wondered what had happened, and I found out when she popped back in and told me that she'd had another

AND THEN THERE WAS ONE

health scare. They'd found something else wrong and she'd had to go back for more treatment. And then she told me some lovely things that I'd never have guessed in a million years.

The lady told me that the first time she'd walked into J7, she'd been petrified. She'd been through the journey of cancer and chemo, and it had taken all her confidence away. Behind those movie-star glasses, and beneath that Audrey Hepburn wig, she'd been terrified.

The woman said that my energy and character had made her feel unafraid for the first time since she'd been ill. She said I was the first person in ages who hadn't wrapped her in cotton wool, and who'd talked to her like she was a normal person. And she'd come back in to thank me. I was so, so touched. I'll never forget it. I knew the health centre was important, but moments like this really summed up the purpose of the space and how it could change people's lives.

I still don't even know her name! I've only seen her once since. I had to go to North Manchester Hospital, round the corner from J7, and I popped into the chippy over the road. She was in there, buying chips, and we had a lovely chat. She is a fantastic woman. I hope she's doing OK.

I remember another disabled client well from the early days because we pissed ourselves laughing all the way through his first session. The guy was about forty and he came in on crutches. He only had his left leg. He was an amputee from the hip because of an illness he'd had as a child. They hadn't amputated his sense of humour, though. He was a proper Manc, taking the piss out of himself, me and everything else. He had me in stitches.

He was super-strong, as well. His upper body was fully able and he could do a lot with it. He was really good at pull-ups and at bench press. But what amazed me, when I sat him down to do some work on his leg, was that he had fantastic flexibility in it. He could really extend it. So I decided to give him a proper challenge.

I got the guy doing squats. *One-legged squats!* Can you imagine? I held his hand to give him support and balance, and he squatted with one leg. Incredible! Then we did bits and bobs with him jumping up and down on the step. He did everything I asked him to do.

Then I had him hopping from one end of the gym to the other. Man, he loved it! His leg was shaking, but he wanted that feeling because he'd never been pushed that way before. It was a wonderful session and he never stopped making sarky quips. We laughed from start to finish.

I never saw that bloke again. He wasn't local anymore: he'd moved up to Burnley, and he'd only come back to visit his family and had decided to come into the gym. I don't know what had made him decide to come in and train. But I still think about that session and it always makes me smile. There's so much focus on what disabled people 'can't' do and yet, that session was only full of 'doing'.

AND THEN THERE WAS ONE

We have to work harder at removing our prejudices. It's amazing what disabled people can do, if they get a chance. I was being shown, time and time again, that all you have to do is give people that chance.

The Audrey Hepburn lady and the guy from Burnley were only passing through J7. It had been a pleasure to train them but they didn't stick around. However, we started getting more and more sick and disabled people in who were becoming consistent, regular visitors. And they quickly became a big part of the J7 family.

One was a woman called Sandra. She had been through a horrible time as she recovered from breast cancer. Working with Sandra was a bit of a stop-start process because her health was fluctuating as she got over the illness. My priority with her was making sure that the atmosphere in J7 was right for her and that it gave her a massive hug.

Sandra had to know that she was accepted and respected and valued in J7. I tried to tell her, and show her, that it was OK to be tired and stressed and emotional some days, due to the effects of the chemo. It was OK to be physically and emotionally up and down. I had to show I'd always accept her and understand what she was going through.

*

By the start of 2020, the centre was thriving. It had established itself in the community, we had tons of people coming in, and I was spending more and more time working with disabled clients. But then, just as I was thinking things could hardly get any better, everything crashed to a halt. Because the world shut down.

I remember the beginning of the first Covid lockdown like it was yesterday. It was a Friday. I was getting ready to take a 6 p.m. class and customers were coming in saying, 'Oh, J, you're going to have to close down.' I was like, *huh?* So, I got on my phone, on the BBC app, and yep, it was saying all facilities like mine would have to shut.

For some reason, I was being cool and positive about it at first. I said, 'Ah, it's all good! We'll have to shut down for a day or two, a week at most, and then we'll be open again.' It was hard to process the gravity of the situation, and it didn't feel serious, or real. But then, after the class had finished, and I was closing up, it hit me.

I was outside, pulling down the shutters. My body started shivering; I don't know why. I put my key in the shutters and suddenly felt really emotional. I broke down crying. Two girls who had just been training in the gym were sitting in a car right behind me. I turned my back, so they couldn't see, and I sobbed my heart out.

I was thinking: *What are my disabled guys going to do? My elderly guys? What will happen to the community we have built here? To the people who rely on it? I know how much this place means to them. I know what it brings to their everyday existence. It brings them joy and happiness.*

AND THEN THERE WAS ONE

It brings them purpose. A lot of people don't have anyone to stand up for them or fight for them. What will they do?

I couldn't hide my feelings. I got in my car and I sobbed. I wasn't able to drive for 20 minutes. And then I realised something, which snapped me out of my funk. I thought: *Of course they're going to be OK. They'll be fine. I'M not going anywhere. THEY'RE not going anywhere. J7 is more than a facility. It's friendship, togetherness, maybe even a way of life. Those guys and I have an unbreakable bond. It could survive an earthquake. We'll come through this. We'll be OK.*

I calmed down, wiped my eyes and drove home.

Covid was a horrible, horrible time. So many people suffered. And so many people lost loved ones. On a day-to-day level, not seeing my guys during lockdown was hard. But we made sure we checked in with each other. There were calls and texts. FaceTimes. I did a lot of Zooms. It was a tricky time but it made me realise, once again, that the power of care and kindness can conquer anything.

I looked after my oldies during lockdown. I delivered more than 300 bags of food to my disabled and elderly clients. When other members of the community heard what I was doing, they started doing the same. They'd bring bags of groceries to me so I could drop them off to older, immunocompromised people who couldn't get out.

Eventually, the law changed and we were allowed to do some outdoor stuff. So, I'd meet some clients every week in a local park and do a big workout. It meant a lot, because some people were struggling mentally during lockdown. Meeting up was the healthiest thing we could do.

*

One crucial development for J7 came about during lockdown. It was a conversation with my brother, Tyrone, and it was all about social media.

At that point, I'd only dabbled in social media. I'd been on Instagram since 2012, and I'd sometimes put up footage of me training people, including some disabled people. But I didn't take it very seriously or think anything of it. It was just a fun thing to do as a little sideline.

I obviously had to respect my clients' privacy. After all, not everyone likes social media, and the most important thing to me is that J7 feels like a safe, inclusive space. Sandra would occasionally let me film our sessions and put a little clip online, but she didn't want me to tag her. It was the same with a couple of my other clients. I'd film us messing about but I made sure you couldn't really tell who anyone was. With their permission, I'd stick those little bits on my Instagram stories with no captions.

It felt like a chance to show people what we were doing at J7, but it wasn't a priority for me at all. It was Tyrone who changed that. He was in my lockdown bubble, and one day he came around, sat me down and had a serious word with me.

AND THEN THERE WAS ONE

'Bro, you've got to properly get onto social media,' he said. 'It's perfect for what you do. What you have got here is so powerful. So many people need inspiration now and you could really share some and make a difference.'

Well, I always take my brother seriously (although he might not think so!) and, after he'd gone, I reflected on his words. *Hmm, maybe Ty is right?* I thought. *When J7 opens again, I'll give social media more of a go. Why not? What have I got to lose?*

We got through it, and when we came out the other side, it made me appreciate our community all the more. It was one of the best days of my life when we got the all-clear and I could put that key back in the shutters and open up again. I was beaming with happiness.

*

In 2021, a young guy named Josh came in. I remember vividly the first time I ever saw him. He was 23. He looked so small, and so innocent, in his wheelchair, and I could see that he was nervous as hell. He wasn't the loudest or the most confident of guys. So, I just tried to make him feel relaxed and make him laugh. I wanted him to feel at home.

His Aunty Lisa made it happen. She worked in Wilkinson's, round the corner from J7, and she'd been watching the videos of me training disabled people that I'd started putting on Instagram. Out of the blue, she sent me a message: 'Would it be OK for my nephew to come and see you?'

When they arrived, it wasn't hard to tell that Josh didn't want to be there, or that he wasn't fond of gyms. I sensed he'd probably been to a gym before, maybe for physio, and hadn't had a good experience. As soon as he came in, I could feel his anxiety. And I figured, *OK, I need to change his mind. Right now.*

My first priority was trying to build trust. I knew Josh had never been in a situation like this before and had probably never been around a man like me, with my voice and energy! Because, let's face it, I know I can be a bit much! I'm loud and I'm silly, and I suppose I'm a bit mad, and I've always been like that. It's just the way I am. So early doors, I knew I needed to get him used to my personality. With all the people I train, it's important that I earn their respect from the outset. And I will go to great lengths to make sure I achieve that.

I'm a big believer in energy. Energy doesn't lie. It's truthful and it's transferable. I know if I give people energy that is real and honest and raw, and I smack them in the face with it, they will absorb it and then give it back to me. I give people my love and my energy and I see that it lifts them up.

I'm not afraid to use my voice. I'm not afraid to show people my feelings and to put everything out there, on the table. I think it encourages them. Every time they see me

AND THEN THERE WAS ONE

being fearless, and unapologetically myself, they think, *I can do that, too.* And when I see people respond to me like that, I feel proud.

I look at the person I'm about to train and I wonder what will lift them up and make them happy. And when I looked at Josh Coy, I saw somebody who longed to get out of his wheelchair. So, I started by doing some basic stuff. I talked to Josh to help him feel relaxed and I had him lifting some weights, to start showing him what he was capable of in the gym. We did a bit of sparring. Then I said I was going to get him out of the chair. He looked so nervous. In fact, I think he said he was nervous! So, I said, 'I'm nervous, too. Let's be nervous together and see what happens!' And I lifted him out of the chair and I held him up, standing, for about 20 seconds. It was one of the best things we ever did.

Josh and I bonded from the start. Our relationship grew so strong, so quickly. He was one of my first disabled clients who properly started coming to J7, week in, week out. He will always be special to me.

One thing I will never forget is the day when Joshy came in and one of the guys who works with me, Badger, and I got him out of his chair – and we went for a run! We supported Josh, one on each side, and he moved his legs as much as he could and ran all around the gym. All the way from reception to the back toilet. He did great, and I told him, 'You know what? You could go further than that!'

YOU ARE NOT YOUR LIMITS

I was thinking about that session afterwards and I had the idea of taking Josh outside the gym, just into the car park. And once I'd had the idea, I couldn't stop thinking about it. I knew it would be the biggest test yet of Josh's fitness, his trust, his belief, his dedication – *everything*. I never doubted that he would give it a go. He's a brave guy. I worried it might cause him to ache afterwards, though!

But then I thought further. I went deeper. I thought, *Josh wants to be treated normally, like everyone else. If I'm training able-bodied people, I push them hard. I push them harder than they think they can go. And, if I'm going to treat Josh normally, I have to do the same with him. I have to give him that choice.*

So, the next time he came in, we started in the gym. I got Josh out of his chair and Badger and I supported him, one on each side. 'Leg it, Joshy!' I told him, and we ran down one side of the gym. I had a chair waiting for him and, as we sat him in it, I broke the bad news.

'I lied to you,' I told him. 'We're gonna go around the gym! Leg it outside!' I yelled. 'Keep going, Josh! You're like a leopard!' And we pegged it outside into the (guess what?) Manchester drizzle.

I had another chair waiting outside, and after about 20 seconds of running, Josh moving his legs as fast as he could, I lowered him onto it. Josh was breathing proper heavy now, and his face was showing the effort . . . but he was still smiling. I pointed to a chair 20 yards away, down the other end of the car park: 'OK, *that's* where we're gonna get to!'

We set off. We had to grab a chair and do an extra stop halfway there, but he made it all the way to the last seat. 'Brilliant, Josh! He's like a gazelle!' I shouted. That made him laugh, although, to be honest, he could probably have done without me singing 'Eye of the Tiger' at him! But that song suits him. Because he *is* as brave as Rocky.

I gave him one last breather and then we finished the circuit, all the way round the outside of the gym and in the back door. I'd rigged up a finishing line from toilet paper and Josh beamed and waved his arms in the air as he breasted it. He'd done it! What a champion!

I always knew he would. I knew he'd finish it, and the joy and happiness and pride he would get from the achievement would outweigh how hard it had been. I thought he'd love it. And he did.

Since then, I have had Joshy out of his chair so many times – every time he comes in, in fact! I've had him holding ropes and bouncing on a trampoline. I've had him doing things that, to an able person, feel normal, but to him feel so, so special. And he absolutely loves it. It liberates him.

When one of my guys does something really big, like Joshy running all the way around the gym, I lavish praise all over them. I really go to town: 'Woah! Wow! Yes, Josh! You've done it, man! Fantastic!' One reason for that, of course, is I want to put some happiness into my brothers and sisters. But, also, I'm totally in awe of them.

A triumph like that *is* huge. I'm a sportsman, so I love amazing achievements in sport. I love watching Michael Jordan or Kobe Bryant playing basketball, or seeing Usain Bolt set a new 100-metre world record. But when I see Josh getting out of his wheelchair and standing up for ten seconds, for me that's on a par with Usain Bolt. I mean it, man! Joshy running all the way around my gym is on the same level as Wayne Rooney scoring a bicycle kick goal.

Josh and I have done so many other great sessions. We've got down on our knees on my orange mats and battled each other with boxing gloves on the ends of poles. I tried to stare Joshy out, so he growled at me like a lion and then he gave me some right clumps around the head with his pole! He put his hands in the air in triumph as I gave up.

I like getting Josh out of his chair and moving around the floor on his hands and knees, because it's great for his mobility. I've set up a finish line – and then piled barbell weight after barbell weight on his back as he's crawled towards it. By the end, he's had six of the beasts weighing him down – proper heavy! He still made it to the end.

Another time, I lay down on the mats with Josh. 'We're two fish trying to get biscuits,' I said, pointing at two packs of biscuits ten feet away.

'They're mine!' he said. As Josh crawled towards them,

AND THEN THERE WAS ONE

I was wrestling him and trying to hold him back. Josh still made it to the biccies before me. What a star! As I said to him then, *'You are not your limits.'* And he knows it.

Social media – Facebook, Instagram, and later, TikTok – has created our J7 superstars. It's given those brave, talented, disabled guys that I train, week after week, an audience of millions. It's let them reach and inspire people all over the globe. And the very first J7 superstar was Josh. He was there right at the start of our social media journey.

Right away, Josh seemed energised by the possibilities that social media offered. I guess maybe because he's a creative guy, he was into the idea of making videos. So, we'd stick a couple of minutes up on Instagram. And he'd go home, pick up his phone, and read hundreds and hundreds of fantastic, encouraging comments:

'Go, Josh!'

'Man, you are amazing!'

'That is the most inspiring thing I've ever seen!'

'You are killing it!'

'Keep it up, Josh! I love you!'

And how must that feel?

Josh has grown so much from the shy, nervous little guy who came in four years ago. He's so much stronger in himself. I've watched him blossom and all of us at J7 couldn't be prouder of him.

YOU ARE NOT YOUR LIMITS

JOSH:

What can I say? It's insane how big the response is. It's crazy, but in a good way. I get home, and I look at Javeno's socials, and we might have 5,000 likes, and hundreds and hundreds of comments, on something that I only did 30 minutes ago! I read them, and it's all, 'Hello from Canada!' 'Hi from Romania!' It's wonderful.

I scroll down and my phone is full of people cheering me on. It's lovely to see. As well as being on Javeno's feeds, I share my sessions on my own socials because I'm always dead proud of what I've done. I try to answer all the messages I get sent but sometimes there are so many that I can't keep track.

The thing is . . . I've always wanted to inspire people. Because my J7 sessions go all over the world, I know that other disabled people see them and think, yeah, I can do that as well! They message me and say they're doing the same as me, and it makes me feel like I've done my job. I've put my stamp on the world. It's beautiful.

And it's all down to Javeno. He brings me confidence, he brings me a healthier lifestyle, he brings me joy. It's so big, I find it hard to put into words. Javeno is such a massive part of my life. He's made me feel so much more confident in myself and what I can do. He's boosted my independence. He's made me feel I can have an impact.

3.
THE OPTIONS ARE LIMITLESS

PAUL:
I was flicking through social media at home one day and I came across one of Javeno's videos. I just thought, wow, this guy is great. He's brilliant. *He's the exact kind of coach I need because, when it comes to training, I know what I need to do, but I need my backside kicking now and again.*

It's 30 miles from where I live to J7 but I drove over to see what he was all about. Javeno was in there, training someone. When he'd finished, I asked him, 'Would it be OK if I came here to do some training with you?' He said, 'Yeah, that should be fine.' So, we fixed up a time, then I turned around and started wheeling towards the door.

YOU ARE NOT YOUR LIMITS

'Oi! Where do you think you're going?' Javeno called after me. I stopped.

'I've not come here to train now,' I answered. 'Just to meet you.'

'Well, you're here now, so you're going to train,' he said. 'Let's see what you can do.'

He got me doing a few weights there and then, and that was how it started. I've been going once a week ever since. It's been brilliant. Javeno and I clicked straight away. I'm an opinionated guy with a big personality and that can intimidate a lot of people. But it's never going to intimidate Javeno. Because he's exactly the same.

I was born with spina bifida, which is a disability of the spinal column where the nerves don't connect properly. It made me paraplegic. My older sister had the same condition. She died 11 weeks before I was born. I was christened when I was two hours old and my parents were told I wouldn't live to the age of 12. I've just turned 60.

I've always been in a wheelchair. I went to special schools until I was ten and then to a mainstream school. That was hard because in those days the education in special schools wasn't great – they never even taught us to write – so when I got to mainstream school, I was a long way behind the other kids. I used to get bullied. But I made a decision that I was

THE OPTIONS ARE LIMITLESS

never going to be a pushover for anybody. So, I made myself into the big, outgoing, outspoken person that I am today. I know I'm not everyone's cup of tea, but that's me. Take me or leave me. I am what I am.

Being in a wheelchair, I grew up being told, 'You can't do that.' And I used to think, you fuckin' watch me and see if I can do it! *The best thing anyone can ever say to me, for motivation, is that I can't do something. Because I will. Maybe not today, maybe not tomorrow, but I'll do it at some point.*

Towards the end of my time in school, I discovered sport. I got invited to a Yorkshire schools disabled sports meeting. I didn't want to go at first, because I was in denial about being disabled. I'd always hung out with able-bodied mates rather than other disabled kids. I only went because it was a day off school.

It was in Huddersfield. I went along and did quite well at everything, but then it got to the wheelchair racing. A guy beat me. I came second. I went back home and I did press-ups and sit-ups every day for a year. The following year, I went back to the same event and I beat him.

That got me into training and going to the local sports centre. At first, they wouldn't let me go on their running track. They said my wheelchair would damage it! In those days, people thought that if you were disabled, you couldn't do anything. But then I got asked to join a disabled sports club.

We entered local competitions and I got better and better. I used to win wheelchair races at 100m, 200m and 400m. Those distances were long enough for me. Daft as it sounds, I was quite lazy. Then someone at the club asked if I'd like to do a marathon. 'Are you joking?' I said. 'It's a long way!'

'It's in Japan.'

'Japan? Yeah, OK, I'll do it!'

My big problem was that I was just in an ordinary wheelchair. I needed a racing chair, but they had to be imported from Germany and they cost £450, which was a heck of a lot of money in the early eighties. In the end, I did a ten-mile sponsored push, from Dewsbury Sports Centre to one in Huddersfield, to raise the funds for it.

Once I had a proper chair, nothing could stop me. I don't want to sound big-headed, but I was a wheelchair racing prodigy. I went to a senior tournament and wiped the floor with everyone, but they wouldn't give me the medals because, technically, I was still a junior. If I'm honest, I'm still quite bitter about that.

I entered national championships and won them all, hands down. I started breaking British records. At one time, I held every single British wheelchair

THE OPTIONS ARE LIMITLESS

racing record, from the 100 metres to the marathon. I began training with the GB disabled sports team and in 1984, when I was 20, I was in the Paralympics.

The able-bodied Olympics were in Los Angeles that year and the disabled games were meant to be in America as well, but that changed and they were in Stoke Mandeville. I got to the final. I didn't win a medal but competing for Great Britain in front of a home crowd was so emotional. I totally get how the athletes at London 2012 must have felt.

I won the World Wheelchair International Games at Stoke Mandeville in 1985, then some medals in Europe, but in 1987 I had a bad accident. It was April Fool's Day, of all chuffin' days. I fell asleep on the floor in front of the fire at home. Because I had no feeling in my legs, I didn't feel my leg catching fire.

When I woke up, one foot was blown up like a balloon. It was a mess. I managed to get onto my knees, but in doing so tore the skin completely off my legs from my knees to the tips of my toes. It did so much damage. My legs had never worked, but now I ended up having to have both of them amputated at the knees.

That accident took me away from training for 18 months. I got the fear of failure. I didn't enter the disabled national championships again until 1990. I'd done no training at all but I had a go at my first pentathlon: the 100 metres, 1,500 metres, shot, discus and javelin. I took to it and I became the national pentathlon champion.

I tried other sports. Basketball. Fishing: I was the national disabled fishing champion twice. I watch Leeds United, for my sins, and a Paralympian who also goes there got me into powerlifting. I became national champion and, for a while, I was the number one in Europe. There was talk of me going to the 2012 Paralympics but they said I was too old.

The truth is, I've spent my entire life trying to prove to people you should never judge a book by its cover. I've been doing it ever since I was a kid. They used to tell me that I shouldn't play football in the street with my mates. I proved them wrong. OK, I was always the goalie, but I still played football in the street with my mates.

I've always known that sport and everything that comes with it – the challenge, the focus, being part of a team, feeling strong, getting better – is an amazing thing. I got into it a bit younger than Paul, but I totally share his drive to keep improving and his understanding of the confidence it gives you. From day one, my big thing in school was sport. That was where my obsession with fitness and physicality started. I loved PE lessons but, outside of that, I got obsessed with doing 100 press-ups every single

THE OPTIONS ARE LIMITLESS

day. Don't worry, I didn't do them all in one go! That might have been asking a lot, at eight years old! But any chance I got – in the playground, or at lunchtime or after school – I'd drop down and do 10 or 15 press-ups. I'd keep a careful count, and by the end of the day I'd always have done 100.

Yeah, I sound like a total nutter, right? But I knew it was good for me. I liked playing tig or British Bulldog in the playground and loved feeling I was the fittest and most agile kid in the game. It wasn't in a 'big ego' way. I didn't want to feel that I was somehow better than my mates. No. Being strong just gave me confidence and purpose.

It wasn't about muscles, or six-packs, or daft stuff like that. Being an athlete made me feel powerful. The more I trained, the more I felt I could walk into a room and look people in the eye. Even as a kid. I was quite small, really, but it made me feel ten feet tall.

You meet some kids nowadays and they never look you in the eye. I can see some of the struggles young people are up against and I want to help empower them. I try to tell them that training can make them feel better about themselves and more confident, confident enough to use their voice and have a conversation. To meet someone else's gaze.

Oddly enough, although I was sports mad, and still am, I was never all that bothered about football. It wasn't my thing. All my mates were either mad Reds, supporting

YOU ARE NOT YOUR LIMITS

Manchester United, or Blues, following City, and I wasn't either. I don't know why. I just wasn't all that fussed.

When I was in my teens, one of my cousins, Trevor, went to London and started playing for Millwall, so I used to say that I supported them. I must have been the only Millwall fan in Manchester! Then Trevor came back up to Manchester for a visit and brought me a pair of Arsenal socks. So, then that was my team: Arsenal.

I'm just as fickle today. I wind up my mates by saying that I support whoever is top of the league. Nowadays, that's normally Man City, so I say I'm a Blue. But the truth is that I don't really care!

I was never about being on the sidelines. I wanted to participate. That's the real joy in exercise, for me. Everyone can participate, no matter what their age or physical limitations. And, in any case, football wasn't my first sporting true love: that was cricket.

I'll tell you now: when I say cricket was my first true love, I *mean* it. As a boy, it was all I thought about. I was totally obsessed with the game. *Totally.* All I wanted to do with my life was to be a top-level professional cricket player.

It all started with my dad. Cricket is obviously the national sport in Jamaica, where I was born and where my parents are from, and Dad was a massive fan. It rubbed off on me. I didn't get into cricket just to please Dad, though; I got into it because I loved playing, but the fact that my dad loved the game, and loved me playing it, was

THE OPTIONS ARE LIMITLESS

important to me. And, again, I wanted to *participate*. I found the energy of the game addictive and couldn't help but want in. I think that's what I saw in Ishmael that day in the park. I recognised that desire to get involved, feel the bat in your hands.

Also, growing up in Manchester in the 1990s, there were a lot of people from different backgrounds, it was very multicultural, but there was also racism. It was tough to take. So, I was grateful that there was a safe space in cricket, a space that existed outside of school. One thing I particularly love about the sport is that people of all ethnic backgrounds play it – and teams of Indian, Pakistani or Afro-Caribbean players regularly win. It's a sport that makes people feel seen.

I'll never forget, when I was about nine, my dad showed me an old VHS tape of the 1976 Old Trafford Test match between England and the West Indies. It was the famous series where, before it started, the England captain, Tony Greig, had said they would make the West Indies 'grovel'. Then the series started and the Windies' fast bowlers *destroyed* 'em!

The West Indies had some amazing fast bowlers back then but the one who made a big impression on me, when my dad showed me the vid, was Michael Holding. *Man, he was fast! He* seemed to start his run-up right on the boundary! I remember asking, 'Dad, why is he running in from right back there?'

YOU ARE NOT YOUR LIMITS

'Shush,' my dad said. 'Listen!'

I did.

'What can you hear?' he asked.

'Nothing!'

'No. Because he's called the Whispering Death.'

Huh? What the heck is the Whispering Death? I concentrated like mad. I still couldn't hear anything. And then, as Holding got to the crease and released the ball . . . I did.

Whoosh! That was the noise the ball made as it left Holding's hand and hurtled towards the England batsman at 95mph. That noise mesmerised me. And that was the exact moment that I got obsessed with fast bowling.

I would watch my dad's tape of that West Indies series over and over again. When Holding bowled, it was like his power was limitless. His confidence was unmatched. He was so fast that the West Indies wicketkeeper, Deryck Murray, had to stand miles behind the wicket and jump in the air to catch the ball when the England batters missed it, as they usually did.

Man! I thought to myself. *I want to bowl as fast as that!*

I'd already started playing cricket at school and now my brother, Tyrone, started to take me to Crumpsall Park to teach me how to bowl. He was a really good batsman, and I'd bowl at him for hour after hour after hour. And now I'd seen the Whispering Death, my run-up got three times longer!

THE OPTIONS ARE LIMITLESS

I'd bowl and bowl and bowl. It was all I wanted to do. Ty and I would play with our cousins and our friends. We'd take it in turns to bowl six-ball overs and we'd all keep our own count of how many balls we'd bowled. Except that when it was my turn, I'd cheat and just keep going. If I wanted to have Holding's kind of confidence, I knew it would take as much practice as possible.

I started playing for my school team in year seven but that wasn't enough. I needed more. I joined Cheetham Hill Cricket Club, just down the road, and played for them at weekends. It's true that practice makes perfect, and I got really, really good at fast bowling.

By the time I was 11, I was playing for Cheetham Hill second team, against fully grown men. And, not to put too fine a point on it, I was *destroying* them. I was running in from miles out and hitting them on the head with bouncers or taking them clean off their feet with yorkers. And it felt brilliant. It was one of the first times in my life when I began to appreciate how sport can make you *feel*.

I loved the tactical side of fast bowling. Working out the strategy. Before I took the ball, I'd think hard about what I had to do, and about my opponent. *I'm going to get you out.* I just had to work out how to do it. Should I bowl a bouncer to scare them, then a straight one to hit the middle stump? I'd visualise the stump flying through the air behind them. And then I'd make it happen. I quickly realised that if I wanted to achieve something, it wasn't enough to believe I could do it, I had to picture myself doing it.

I was completely devoted to cricket. Nothing could distract me from it – which turned out to be a very good thing on one occasion in particular. I remember one Friday evening, after school, going to a barber in Cheetham Hill to get a haircut (I still get it cut in the same shop today). A bunch of lads from the estate were in there and they tried to get me to go down the park with them later.

'Jav, bruh, it's gonna be wicked!' they were all saying. 'We've got drinks and smokes and some girls are coming down. You've got to come!'

'Nah, man, I've got a match in the morning,' I said. 'I'm taking five wickets tomorrow so I need an early night!'

But they wouldn't let up: 'Fuck that, Jav, man, come down!' They were begging me.

I was laughing and joking with them, but it felt awkward: how many times can you say no? But I didn't budge. I knew I needed to be all in or all out.

In the end, I was glad I didn't go. As it turned out, there was a load of trouble in the park that night. It all kicked off big time. One of the lads got stabbed and another got shot. Two of the boys were arrested and ended up being locked up for a very long time. It's scary to think what might have happened to me if I had gone. I hope you understand what I mean when I say that I felt as if cricket had saved me. It gave me a focus and a reason to keep going.

THE OPTIONS ARE LIMITLESS

*

Back then, Cheetham Hill had a pretty bad reputation. It was notorious for stuff like gang violence and feuds with Moss Side. When people in nicer areas of Manchester heard the words 'Cheetham Hill', it didn't get a great response. And the way outsiders judged our whole community was threatening to affect my cricketing ambitions.

By my early teens, I was getting to be the star player at Cheetham Hill Cricket Club. I was a ferocious fast bowler who was sending wickets flying every week. I had a great coach called Frank Connolly who was writing to Lancashire County Cricket Club about me. He kept telling them, 'Look, I've got this young fast bowler, Javeno McLean, who is unbelievable – you need to come and see him!' But the scouts didn't come, and they didn't even respond to his letters. This went on for nearly two years. Why? Because of where we were. Because of the area's reputation.

I can remember crying because I wanted to be a cricketer so much. I wanted to play for Lancashire more than anything in the world. I was sitting there, crying, thinking, *I'm really good – why won't they come to see me?* But I wasn't going to give up. I don't believe in giving up. Never have. I knew that any scout who saw me would know I was good enough to play professionally. And even if they didn't think I was good enough, I'd soon be able to change their minds. If I wanted them to believe in me, I'd have to show just how much I believed in myself.

I had a word with myself and I made a decision: 'OK, Lancashire won't come down to see me? Then I need to become so good that they have no choice. I have to get so good that they'll see past their prejudices and realise what they are missing out on.' And I did it. The next season, I went absolutely crazy.

I was bowling so fast, it was ridiculous. I was even surprising myself! Every match, every weekend, I was taking stupid amounts of wickets. Even when I suffered an injury, I still turned up at the club and said, 'I'm playing!' and bowled a load of guys out. And it worked. Lancashire took note.

For the first time, the county club sent a scout down to Cheetham Hill. He watched me bowling like a teenage Whispering Death and he was blown away. 'How come we've never seen him before?' he asked my coach, Frank.

'Huh?!' said Frank. 'I've been trying to tell you about him for two years!'

It was an example of how quick we are, as a society, to disregard someone or question their value, often because of factors beyond their control, whether it's something like a postcode or even a disability.

In 1999, Lancashire signed me up to play for their under-15 juniors team. *Yes! This was what I wanted*! It was a big thrill. I started training with them at weekends and

THE OPTIONS ARE LIMITLESS

playing games in the summer during school holidays. It was a big step up from matches for my school or Cheetham Hill, but I wasn't fazed. I'd worked hard for this and I still had my self-confidence.

*

Cricket taught me a lot of lessons. It taught me about work ethic, respect and manners. Yet it also taught me that things don't always work out the way you might have hoped. After five years of playing for the club, I realised my future wouldn't be with Lancashire.

I was still bowling up a storm, but I felt less sure I'd get my big breakthrough. I remember playing a match at Liverpool Cricket Club.

There was a big crowd and I had a storming match. I should have had a hat trick: I took two wickets back to back, but when the batsman nicked the third ball to the slips, our fielder dropped it. Even so, I got Man of the Match, and the captain told me to lead the team off at the end, with everyone clapping me.

I got back into the dressing room and waited for our coach to say, 'Well done!' But he didn't. He didn't look at me once. He even walked right past me a couple of times without saying a word. The other players were puzzled. They were asking me, 'What's going on? Is he not going to congratulate you?'

I went home and told Dad what had happened, and

we decided to write a letter to the county. We said that I was a Lancashire lad and that all I wanted to do was to play for Lancashire. We asked if I was ever going to get the chance. The club wrote back but didn't say anything helpful. So, knowing that progression was uncertain, that was it. I left.

It was a big blow, sure, but I still wanted to be a professional cricketer. That was still my dream. I wasn't going to let anything hold me back. I'd had a few rival counties who were interested in me sniffing around, so I began going for a few trials.

Damian D'Oliveira got in touch with me. Damian was the son of a true cricket legend. His dad was Basil D'Oliveira, a brilliant batsman and bowler for Worcestershire and England. Basil was mixed race, and in 1968, when he got picked to tour apartheid South Africa with England, he was refused entry to the country. The tour got cancelled.

Damian was now academy director at Worcestershire and invited me for a trial. It went dead well. He loved my speedy bowling and he offered me a playing opportunity for the 2004/5 season. So, I started commuting on the train from Manchester to Worcester for training sessions and academy matches.

Unlike my previous experience, Damian took an interest in me and showed a lot of faith in my capability. But a strange thing happened at Worcestershire. Despite this new welcoming environment and the fact that I had

THE OPTIONS ARE LIMITLESS

been in love with cricket ever since Dad had shown me the Whispering Death, I started to fall out of love with the game.

A lot of it was down to the attitude of some of the players around me. I've always loved pushing my body and mind to the limit and beyond. I love battling injuries or setbacks and coming back better and stronger. Being a dedicated athlete is life-or-death to me. I have to care about what I do and give it everything I have. But some other players didn't feel the same.

When I looked around the dressing room I saw sportsmen who were crazily talented, but some of them didn't train to the same level as I did, and it broke my heart. I was training insanely hard to be the best athlete, the best cricketer, that I could be. And some of them seemed to be in it for the money, the glitz and the glamour.

I've never got out of bed just for money. You can't chase money. You're never gonna catch it! If you're doing something just for the money, it will become draining. I didn't want to feel like I was just going through the motions. I wanted to be in an environment that made me feel *inspired*. So, at the end of the season, I wasn't sure if I was going to stay at Worcestershire.

So, what next?

Even though I no longer wanted to be a top-level cricketer, I still loved the sport and wanted to find a way to keep it in my life. I started playing local league matches

YOU ARE NOT YOUR LIMITS

for Ramsbottom Cricket Club, just outside Bury. And, through them, I got offered a brilliant opportunity.

*

In 2006, Ramsbottom signed the fantastic Indian cricketer Sunil Joshi as their overseas professional player. Sunil was a great batsman and a fabulous left-arm spin bowler who had played tons of tests and one-day internationals for India. I couldn't believe my luck, getting to play with such an incredible player.

As well as being a cricketing superstar, Sunil was also a wonderful, wonderful man. I took every chance I could to talk to him and learn from him. Then, one day when we were in conversation in the dressing room, he offered me a one-year contract to go to India with him to play for his team, Karnataka.

Man! What an opportunity! I was never going to say no. To think I went from feeling stuck at Lancashire to feeling uninspired at Worcester to travelling to India! That was a transition I could never have anticipated. It just goes to show what changing your environment and staying true to your values can do. So, in autumn 2007, I flew out to India to try to help Karnataka win their domestic league, the Ranji Trophy.

What an adventure! *It. Was. Wild.* Karnataka are based in Bangalore (now called Bengaluru) and they are one of the biggest teams in India, probably only behind Mumbai.

THE OPTIONS ARE LIMITLESS

This meant they could attract some of the country's biggest stars. Suddenly, I was sharing a dressing room with these cricket legends who I'd only ever seen on telly before.

'Toby' has always been my family nickname – even now, my family still call me Toby – and it carried over into my cricket life. When Sunil Joshi introduced me to all those guys at Karnataka, that was what he called me. They could not have been more welcoming. I don't get too overawed around famous people but it blew my little mind every time Anil Kumble, *the captain of India*, said, 'Hey, Toby, you alright? Can I have a word with you?' I don't think he knew how much it meant to me. In that team, no matter how experienced or inexperienced you were, you were treated as an equal.

Karnataka played in a fantastic sprawling ground called the M. Chinnaswamy Stadium, which held 30,000 people and got used for Test matches. Bro, it was a bit of a change from playing for Ramsbottom!

At first, I struggled with the beggars in India. They'd put out their hands for rupees and if I didn't have any, or shook my head, they'd often get quite aggressive. Failing to understand their position, I'd snap at them. Then, one day, I talked about it to a teammate at Karnataka. He explained the context to me and everything fell into place.

'Toby, just think about it,' he said. 'These guys are on the street because of the class system here in India. They have no choice. If it was you, what would *you* do?'

YOU ARE NOT YOUR LIMITS

I listened and, straight away, I got it. I thought, *yeah, if I was on the street, and I had a baby to feed, and I saw a smartly dressed guy, obviously from abroad, with a nice watch on, I'd ask for two rupees. And if he said no, I'd ask again harder.* My teammate's words humbled me. And they changed my behaviour.

I didn't treat beggars as if they were annoying or snap at them anymore. I treated them like fellow human beings. I'd give them what money I had. If I didn't have any on me, I'd say, 'Sorry, I've got nothing now, but next time I come past, I'll give you some.' And I always did.

Playing for Karnataka was amazing. The heat was a real challenge – and it pushed me to play in ways I hadn't before. It taught me resilience, care and how to cope with setbacks. It's safe to say I was humbled on a few occasions! While I wasn't the best player, I was physically the strongest, and this meant I got to coach some of the youth players.

I loved it . . . and I put them through hell! I was so delighted to see, after just a few months, that the guys had all become so much more athletic.

Training those young guys elevated and liberated me. It showed me I could get much more out of helping them than I could get from simply working on myself. It was a massive turning point. Karnataka didn't end up winning the Ranji Trophy, but I had a wonderful time in India. And I flew home knowing so much more about the person I was and the life I wanted to lead.

THE OPTIONS ARE LIMITLESS

I'd always thought that cricket was my true love, but I was wrong. Dead wrong. Cricket was just my first love. My *true* love was helping people.

*

There are three qualities that I swear by: Connection, Trust and Belief. I call them CTB. CTB is like a mantra for me. If you get them all right, in the gym or outside it, you can release people's unstoppable nature. The work I did when I was training those young professional cricketers in India definitely solidified this for me, but so did training ordinary people in Manchester. It doesn't matter who you are training or what they are trying to achieve, it all comes back to CTB. I would say this defines my relationship with Paul, the guy you met at the beginning of this chapter.

Paul is a bit different from my other superstars. He's older and he's been in gyms his entire life. He's in a wheelchair and he's a double-leg amputee from the knees, but that has never stopped him achieving unbelievable things in the world of sport. Paul has been to the very top of a mountain. He's a former Paralympian.

But those incredible achievements can bring their own problems. Paul is a very proud Yorkshireman. Now that he's older, it can be difficult for him to accept that he's no longer able to do everything he used to do. It can be tough to come to terms with the fact that he's no longer 18 and he's not a current Paralympian.

YOU ARE NOT YOUR LIMITS

But in my eyes, Paul will *always* be a Paralympian and nobody can take that away from him. He'll always be an athlete – he still *is* an athlete – and with the CTB that we have between us, we can still do the most incredible things.

As we get older, we all compare ourselves to who we were when we were younger – and Paul is no different. He says things like, 'I used to do this,' and 'I used to be able to do that.' Every session, I'll say to him, 'Yeah, what you did back then was brilliant, mate. And now you're just a different version of that same person.'

I just want Paul to be comfortable in his own skin. Comfortable in the skin of the person he is now. To be grateful for the person he is today.

Paul does the most unbelievable things during our training. I've had him dragging heavy weights around the car park and shoulder-pressing incredible amounts. Recently, he's pushed a tyre that weighs over 200kg: the largest one in the UK. He does stuff that able-bodied men 30 years younger than him couldn't dream of doing.

I've sat opposite Paul, held a bar up, and had him throw a medicine ball over that bar and into my chest, so that it rolled down a cushion in my lap and back to Paul for him to do it again. And again. And again. I held the bar higher and higher, and Paul just kept clearing it. His upper-torso strength is incredible.

It's that thing again: even at his age, with his disability,

THE OPTIONS ARE LIMITLESS

Paul will always be an athlete. Even if he doesn't think so. It's a state of mind. It's the way you live your life. It's about keeping an athlete's mindset, even if your muscles aren't as strong as they once were. I just remind Paul that he will always be an athlete, and he needs to *carry himself like one*.

For a man who's achieved so many wonderful things, Paul can be very hard on himself. He gets really frustrated with stuff like the lack of mobility in his arms. But, as I said earlier, frustration is still a valuable feeling, because it fuels us to turn pain into purpose. I'm always ready to reassure him that he's doing OK – and that training is not about being perfect. It's a safe space to make mistakes because training gives you a way to learn from those mistakes.

Our health centre's culture is based on variety and challenge. Everybody in there challenges the norm every single day. I'm so proud of the culture we have built, and I think it is the reason we get such great results.

When you train properly, in the right environment, with people who care, it teaches you how to really express your emotions. And if people are true to their deepest emotions, the sacrifices they make as they train, physically and mentally, can be very rewarding. Far more rewarding than losing a few pounds, gaining a bit of strength, or gaining movement in your hand.

Paul goes through emotional ups and downs, and I can see why. Navigating life as a disabled or disadvantaged person isn't easy. It can be so hard to feel motivated; to change your habits; simply to *survive*. It's exhausting.

PAUL:

Not that long ago, I was ill and I was stuck at home on my own for a week. I was in bed for three days. It was just me and the dog: I didn't see another soul for the whole week. And I was feeling very, very sorry for myself. I was lying there, thinking, I'm past it. Mate, you're 60 years old. Is doing all this training worth it? I mean, is it really?

The next week, I went back to J7. I took Javeno to one side and I told him, 'I'm thinking of jacking all this in. Knocking it on the head.' What did he do? He went absolutely bananas.

If I'm honest, I don't go to the centre for the equipment. I train in nearer, bigger gyms that have far more choice. I go to J7 purely for Javeno and what I get out of training with him. He gets me fitter, which is what I need, and his training is so versatile. He always thinks up good stuff for me to do. Since I've lost my legs, my balance isn't great, and I can find it hard to stay put on narrow gym benches. Javeno thinks up brilliant ways to get around that, ways that would never have occurred to me.

We once did a session where Javeno was getting me to put a weights bar on top of a stack of chairs.

THE OPTIONS ARE LIMITLESS

He kept stacking them up until they were higher than my head and I kept lifting the bar on top. That video has over 15 million views on TikTok. But I didn't think it was that big a deal. Back in the day, I used to bench press over 200kg. Although I couldn't do that now.

I see the work Javeno does with the younger disabled people at J7 and it's absolutely out of this world. I never had anyone like him when I was that age, and I really wish I had. Because I think it would have made so much difference for me.

When people make you feel included as a kid, it enhances your self-respect and self-love by a million. He builds a confidence in those kids that they might not have gained without him. Javeno tells them they can be who they want to be, whatever disability they may have, and he makes that true.

4.
IF YOU BUILD IT, THEY WILL COME

BRENDA:

After I had my hip replacements, when I was 62, I had some physiotherapy and they advised me to join a gym. I'd heard about the Active Lifestyles classes that Manchester City Council were starting so I went along to one near me. It cost 50p per week. And I was the only person there.

I met Javeno and he was lovely. I'd never been to a gym in my life or done any exercise. It was like learning a foreign language. When Javeno started talking about 'burpees', I didn't have a clue what he was on about. I must have been hard work because he had to talk me through everything, bit by bit. But he was very patient.

YOU ARE NOT YOUR LIMITS

Javeno taught me all the moves. We started off with a chair, and me just sitting down and getting up. It was all about mobility. Then we moved on to doing squats. He worked me quite hard but made it fun, so I didn't always realise how hard I was working. He understood what my limitations were and worked within them.

He was quite quiet when I first met him. Hard to believe, isn't it?! He was very polite and respectful at first because he didn't know me. I remember him asking me, 'Do you mind if I touch your shoulder while I teach you this move?' He's not nearly as polite with me nowadays! I said, 'Luv, you just show me what to do and I'll do it.'

Even though the classes were great, I was still the only person there. Then we changed venue and I started telling friends how good Javeno was. A few of them started coming with me. We gradually got more and more people. And then it just exploded.

I started doing weekend and school holiday sports coaching sessions for Manchester City Council when I was 16. I loved it from day one. The council trained me to coach cricket and football, then kept offering me more courses: 'Do you want to do athletics next? Basketball?' I always said yes. The options were limitless. It was ace.

When I returned to Manchester from India at the

IF YOU BUILD IT, THEY WILL COME

beginning of 2008, I threw myself back into running sports training courses for the council. I trained harder than ever and took on anything that was available. Everything they offered me, I did (even when I knew nothing about the sport). 'Badminton? Yeah, nice one, let me at it!'

Coaching the young players at Karnataka had really whetted my appetite for physical training. And, suddenly, I got the chance to train more people than ever. Manchester City Council was refocusing its sports activity department more towards health and wellbeing in the community. They rebranded it as 'Active Lifestyles'. I'd been doing stuff for the council for six or seven years by now, and they offered me the post of head exercise specialist within the new department.

The role was basically to get Manchester active. I had to create, and deliver, exercise classes all over the city, targeting all sorts of demographic groups, ranging from young people to minority-ethnic communities, disadvantaged people and the elderly. Needless to say, I jumped at the chance.

Having decided to stop being an elite cricketer, this job was ideal for me. It combined the two main interests that have motivated me all my life: sport and community. And, though I didn't know it at the time, it would also enable me to discover my other great passion: helping disabled people.

From day one, I loved my new role. I started organising

all sorts of sessions. Circuit training, kettlebell classes, mobility classes, OAP classes, aerobics, Pilates, running groups. I wanted to provide a variety of options so everyone could find something that worked for them. A lot of the classes were group sessions but a few were one-to-ones. If a class was needed, I'd set it up. I was doing everything I could to get Manchester fitter. Devising these classes and sessions, and seeing people grow stronger and more confident in themselves in front of my eyes, week by week, was magic.

I particularly loved that I was mostly working in quite poor communities. Over the years, I've worked in all sorts of places, and in wealthier areas I think you can get a lot of pretence. Poor communities are different. You see truth and effort and real, raw emotions. You see people who may not have much money and may not be in the best of health, but who are trying, *really* trying, to improve and be healthier and more active. It made me – no, it *still* makes me – feel great when I can help those people on their path.

In my head, I contrasted them with the professional cricketers I'd seen messing about in the changing room, not bothering to train, just taking their pay cheques. The people I was working with didn't have smart kit, or much confidence, but they were giving it their all. And I knew who I preferred.

But that doesn't mean that every course I set up was

IF YOU BUILD IT, THEY WILL COME

an unqualified success from day one. In 2010, I started a fitness class, open to anybody, at a school in North Manchester. To be honest, it wasn't a great venue. It was a bit hard to get to and, when you did get there, the hall was freezing cold. And for months and months, only one person turned up for the class. But that was OK, because she was a very special person.

Brenda was a lady in her sixties who had just had two hip operations. She hadn't let that get her down, though. She and I got on like a house on fire. Her banter wasn't that of a typical pensioner, I'll tell you that for nothing!

It was basically a circuit training class, but I'd mix it up and make it different every week. It might be seated exercises, it might be body-weight stuff, it might be ball work. We did everything. And I never once went into the session thinking, *oh, it's only one older lady.* I gave the class everything, every single week. And, most importantly, so did Brenda.

Aware that this class was undersubscribed, to say the least, the council wanted to put out flyers to drum up interest, but I said no, because I wanted people to hear by word of mouth how good the classes were. A personal recommendation holds so much more weight than a general information leaflet. And Brenda did that. She started telling her mates. She got four or five people coming down at first, and then we had 20, and then 30. We moved to a bigger venue that could accommodate 40 or 50 people, and then we had to move again, to my old school, Our Lady's Roman Catholic High School in Blackley.

The class just kept growing until it was 130 or 140 people, every Tuesday and Thursday night. There were so many participants that I had to get a few people in to help me: two trainers, Siobhan and Catherine, and my little cousin, Phil. And that huge class was where I first learned to perform and to organise people. It was proof that the demand was there; we just had to reach those people.

I didn't use a microphone – just my voice. Luckily, I've got a very big voice! The class was made up of all sorts: men, women, young people, OAPs, even professional sportspeople. Brenda (who I now always called 'Queen Brenda') was there. My mum was in the class! And I was legging it up and down the room, trying to give everyone a great shared experience.

For me, that's the trick to taking a successful exercise class. The shared experience. It's not about an individual having a great moment. It's about everyone doing something together, sharing the energy. That's where the power is: in creating communal experiences that belong to all of us. It's less scary that way: what starts off as an intimidating exercise class suddenly becomes an uplifting social space where you can prioritise your health and motivate others.

So I'd be running around the room like a nutter, getting everyone going, trying to share the energy. I'd peg it up and down, making sure they were all alright, ensuring no

IF YOU BUILD IT, THEY WILL COME

one felt left out. I had something to say to everyone in the session.

'You alright? How you getting on at work?'

'How's your mum? Nice one!'

'Is your dog OK now? Great!'

I wanted to make sure that not one person left the class feeling that I hadn't interacted with them. And we all had a bloody great time. Sometimes it felt more like a party than a gym class.

So, it was totally ironic that this was the point when I managed to knacker myself with a horrible sports injury. I went down the local leisure centre with Tyrone to play squash. I was really enjoying the game, mainly because I was totally smashing him up! Then, as I played a shot by the wall, I heard a loud CRACK and I dropped to the floor.

For a second, I didn't know what had happened. It felt like something had hit the back of my leg. 'Did someone just throw something at me?' I asked Ty.

'No, bro,' he said. 'I heard a noise, but I thought it was your racquet hitting the wall.'

'I never hit the wall!' I said.

And then I looked down at my leg.

My calf muscle was virtually detached from the bone. It was hanging on by a thread. And suddenly I was in agony. The pain was excruciating. I got rushed to hospital, where they told me that I had snapped my Achilles tendon and they needed to operate.

YOU ARE NOT YOUR LIMITS

After the op, I had to wear a massive space boot. The docs told me I wouldn't be able to do any sport for at least six months. I felt desperate. *Six months! There's no way I can go six months without training! I'll go mental! And what about my job?*

The very next morning, I went to my local gym.

It was up three flights of stairs, 60 steps in total, and I hobbled up them on my crutches in my space boot. The pain was horrific, but I got all the way to the top, and then I did 250 pull-ups. I trained every day of those six months I was supposed to be laid up. I'm not saying that's the right thing to do, but it's what felt right for me at that moment. Movement was so important to my mental health and I knew I would have to find a way to include it without delaying my recovery. It was an eye-opening experience: it was the first time I'd trained with a serious injury and it required a completely different level of mental energy.

Luckily, I was also able to carry on doing my new job. Manchester City Council were great and stood right by me. They proved themselves to be an inclusive workplace, offering to pay for taxis to get me to all my classes. Not only did it mean I got to carry on doing what I loved, it meant the classes could still run for the benefit of others. I didn't want to let anybody down.

*

IF YOU BUILD IT, THEY WILL COME

The nature of my job was that I planned the sessions, but I wasn't taking all of them myself. That wouldn't have been possible. Some of them I was just managing or supervising. One early session that really sticks in my mind was with a young disabled lad in a wheelchair in Wythenshawe Leisure Centre.

The kid was evidently really strong. His dad was with him: a big, bald guy with tattoos who looked a bit like an aging rocker. And he was watching his son being given the dullest exercise class you can imagine. The coach training the lad had no energy, no performance, no love, no care. Nothing. He was just mumbling at him. There was no connection. And the kid in the wheelchair looked bored stupid.

While the trainer popped to the loo, I watched the lad stand up out of his wheelchair and get himself a glass of water. I thought, *I've had enough of this.* When the coach came back in, I told him to go and get a cup of tea: I was taking the rest of the class. I went over and spoke to the kid.

'Listen!' I said. 'Don't ever let anybody dilute you. Don't let anybody say to you that this wheelchair defines you. Don't let anybody take your power. I have just watched you, for half an hour, doing nothing. You're lifting little weights but you can do so much more.'

The lad stared at me. He didn't have a clue what to say.

'This is what we're going to do,' I continued. 'You're going to stand up.'

YOU ARE NOT YOUR LIMITS

He got up out of his wheelchair.

'You've been doing bicep curls with 1kg weights. How about we try the 2kg or the 3kg? I don't know if you can do it. If you can, we're winning. If you can't, you'll go down trying. But you're not going to stay at level one when I *know* you've got other levels to explore.'

I handed him the 2kg weights. He lifted them easy. I gave him the 3kgs. Easy again. I gave him the 4kgs and it was a bit more of a challenge, but he gave it a good go. He got tired, we took a break where he sat down to have a drink, and then we went on to shoulder presses. I pushed him hard.

The session ended and the lad's dad walked over to me. The giant of a man covered in tattoos, who I'd clocked earlier, was now in front of me, crying. Proper weeping. And he gave me a hug that smothered me! I disappeared!

'I've never seen somebody treat my son the way you just did,' he told me. 'The way you spoke to him is just what me and his mum want. We want the world to treat him normally and you're the first person to do it. As parents, that's all we want. Thank you.'

It reminded me of Ishmael playing cricket in Cheetham Hill Park all those years ago and his wife hugging me afterwards. I've realised, over the years, that what that man said is almost always true: all the loved ones of disabled people want is for their family member to be treated normally. It's such a basic thing, but so many people don't do it.

IF YOU BUILD IT, THEY WILL COME

I spoke to that coach afterwards and told him: 'Treat people like humans. Notice them. Don't over-complicate it and don't mollycoddle them. What you did, accidentally, was put that young man in a box: *oh, he's disabled*. He doesn't want that. He's like anybody: he wants to be treated normally. So, treat him that way.'

When I'd seen that kid in his wheelchair, I hadn't seen the chair. I'd seen the kid. I'd seen a kid who was being lazy, who was being *allowed* to be lazy, and who needed pushing. So, I'd done it. It was nothing. But, at the same time, it was monumental. And that's what I do now to every disabled person who comes through the door of my gym.

*

I got so much satisfaction out of my job with Manchester City Council. The level of fulfilment I was getting was unreal. I absolutely loved meeting people of all ages, shapes and sizes, getting to know them, and seeing their fitness levels ratchet up and up. It was ace. The money was good, and the council treated me brilliantly and gave me all the resources they could. Their vision for getting Manchester fit and active was magnificent, and I totally bought into it. I worked for them, implementing this programme, for the next ten years. It helped that I had such a brilliant boss, a woman called Sarah who understood me, and got what I was about, from day one.

YOU ARE NOT YOUR LIMITS

There's a great Netflix documentary about Michael Jordan, called *The Last Dance*. It's about Jordan's career, and particularly about his last years with the Chicago Bulls in the NBA. No joke, I watch it every week because it is so inspirational. And my favourite bit of the doc is about Dennis Rodman.

Rodman is quite a weird guy, which can overshadow the fact that he is one of the most amazing basketball players ever. But he's also a party animal: he used to go out with Madonna. And halfway through the 1998 season, with the Bulls pushing for the National Basketball Association title, he told Phil Jackson, their coach: 'I need a break. I need to go and party.'

The rest of the team couldn't believe it. They were all saying, 'What the hell? Dude, we're going for the championship! You need to be here with us!' But Rodman kept on saying, 'I need to go and party.' And Phil Jackson told him, 'OK. I'll give you 48 hours.' Because he knew that, for Dennis to be Dennis, he had to do what he had to do.

So, in the middle of the season, Dennis Rodman went off to Las Vegas. He partied. He got drunk. He met up with Hulk Hogan and did World Championship Wrestling with him. His Bulls teammates were all training hard, then they turned on the TV and saw Rodman, in Vegas, hitting someone with a chair in a WCW fight. They were like, *what the fuck?*

The media were going crazy. It was all over the papers.

IF YOU BUILD IT, THEY WILL COME

They slaughtered Jackson, the coach: 'How the hell could you let him go wild in the middle of the season?' And then Dennis Rodman came back and played the next game and he was unbelievable. He was man of the match. And afterwards, he just said, 'Phil knew I had to do that, for me.'

In a funny way, my manager Sarah was just the same. She knew what made me tick and she trusted me. I remember one time I was on the computer at work, researching burpees and squats. Sarah came over and asked, 'What are you doing?' And I said, 'I need to work out 25 variations of burpees and 25 variations of squats.'

She could see I was 100 per cent into it. There was a major departmental meeting about to start, which I was due to be in, but Sarah just told me, 'OK, carry on.' She let me miss the meeting. Everybody was asking her, 'Where's Javeno? He's supposed to be here.' But Sarah just told them, 'He's doing something.'

It was also Sarah who backed me when I wanted to get a disabled exercise coaching qualification, even though the council weren't doing any specific work with disabled people in this way. She just *got* me. Her belief in me let me focus completely on doing my job to the absolute best of my ability. It's something I've always tried to remember. And, while I wasn't fully aware of it at the time, she was setting me up to become the coach I am today. She is still a very dear friend.

So, when the time came that I was ready to make the

leap and open J7, Sarah didn't try to talk me out of it, though I know a lot of people might have seen it as a risk. I was giving up a good, well-paid job for what was basically a leap in the dark. I know that others at the council were surprised when I quit. I'd been there ten years, the programme was in good nick and the classes were packed, so some of them thought, *why*?

But I just *knew* that if I was true to myself, and I put everything I could into my dream, it would work. Mind you, when I said that to a few people, they looked at me as if I was big-headed. Or mad.

But there's my self-belief again for you . . .

And there was something else that convinced me it was the right time to put my plan into action. It was the arrival of our first son. My wife Laura gave birth to Mason McLean on 7 January 2015, three days after I turned 30. I loved becoming a dad. It was wonderful: the greatest gift ever. It felt as if the puzzle pieces of my life were all falling into place. Becoming a dad made me want to do great things. It was time to become the person I claimed I was. I mean, it was all very well to think of myself as a go-getter, and a risk-taker, but what had I actually *done*?

Even if I'm in a room full of 200 people all saying 'No', if I am saying 'Yes', I will back myself. I had all these ideas, thoughts, feelings and positivity in my head. Now it was time to make use of them. I had to take my vision of a health and fitness centre for everyone and turn it into a reality.

IF YOU BUILD IT, THEY WILL COME

Understandably, Laura was a bit worried about me giving up the security of a regular, well-paid job when we had a new baby, but she stood by me. She's always been supportive. She saw that I wanted to do good things that my new son, and my family, could be proud of.

And, sure enough, when I opened J7, a lot of my clients from Active Lifestyles came along. And Queen Brenda was one of them. In fact, she's the only person who's got a lifetime membership to the gym. Because she's been there, with me, right from the start. And even before.

While Covid was going on, I trained Queen Brenda, in the park, to do 100 squats in a day. When I first suggested it, she looked at me as if I was insane. Actually, she often looks at me like that! But she got sponsored to do it for the Teenage Cancer Trust. Unsurprisingly, she worked like mad, and she did it. She raised a lot of money for them. She's absolutely amazing. Queen Brenda is a prime example of how success doesn't lie in the exercise itself, but in how it empowers you to live your life. If you can show that level of commitment to yourself in your exercise sessions, you can take that self-belief wherever you go.

BRENDA:
I had followed Javeno every time he changed venues for his classes for Manchester City Council. We must have gone to three or four different places, over the

years. And when he opened J7, I followed him there as well.

I loved it from the second I saw it. I'd always thought of gyms as daunting. I remember once, at a local leisure centre, just walking through a gym, and it felt so cold. Everyone was staring at me. It didn't feel friendly. But J7 isn't like that. It's not one of those posing gyms. Everybody is so friendly and they all look out for one another.

I live on my own and I go to J7 three times a week now. I do two group classes and, on Friday mornings, I do a one-to-one session. It's like going to a family, really. Whatever time I go, I always know somebody there. Everyone is very welcoming – and they'll sit and chat. It's a lifeline, really. It stops me feeling isolated.

Javeno cares about everybody who goes to the gym. He keeps an eye on everyone, to make sure they're not over-stretching themselves. But I'll tell you what; if he knows you can do something, and you're slacking, he won't let you get away with it! He's brought a lot of joy to my life. He's a big character and, without him, the world would be a poorer place.

He's got a special name for me now. He calls me Queen Brenda. Mind you, he calls me a few other things, an' all . . .

5.
IT TAKES A VILLAGE

JOANNE:

During the Queen's Platinum Jubilee in 2022, I went to a big celebration concert in Manchester. They were giving away free tickets on Good Morning Britain. *Mark Owen from Take That was playing, and Steps, and Javeno got given an award. I was, like,* I know him! *Because I used to go to his Manchester City Council Active Lifestyles classes.*

They showed some clips at the concert of the work that Javeno was doing now with disabled kids. And as soon as I saw them, I thought, right, I'm going to contact him on Messenger. *Because I knew that what Javeno was doing would be perfect for my 19-year-old son, DJ.*

DJ was born with Down syndrome. He went to a

mainstream primary school and then a special needs high school, but he's always been dead positive his entire life. His biggest problem is his speech, and people understanding what he's saying. But he loves to keep fit: he's really into his fitness. I thought Javeno might be able to push him.

Javeno told me to bring him down to J7. I remember we went after I'd taken DJ to watch them filming the TV show Ninja Warriors. I told Javeno, 'Look, mate, DJ wants to be on that show, so you'd better help him!'

Javeno was – how shall I put this? Very down to earth. He told DJ, 'Right, let's see what you can do, then.' He got him doing press-ups with a clap. DJ was good at it, and Javeno was effing and blinding: 'Oh my God, fucking look at him! He's brilliant!' They were on the same wavelength, a match made in heaven, right from the start.

I knew Javeno would be brilliant for DJ, so I asked how much he would charge to train him.

Javeno looked at me as if I'd just insulted him. 'Fuck off, Joanne!' he said. 'I'm not taking a penny off you!'

Ever since I was young, I've always aimed high and sought to achieve good things. I'm proud of a lot of things I've done in my life, but right up there is the work I've done with J7's superstars. I'm proud that, together, we

IT TAKES A VILLAGE

have made this brilliant space at J7 where everyone is welcome, and that the work we do means people feel seen and valued. I'm not exaggerating when I say that it means *everything* to me.

I'm proud of our laughs together. It breaks my heart the number of disabled people who've said to me, 'Jav, I can't remember the last time I laughed.' They might have forgotten how to smile, and now they remember what a real smile is. Because laughing and smiling is what being alive and being human is all about, right?

Sometimes amazing people come to me via a weird, roundabout route. One of them is a brilliant guy with Down syndrome, called DJ. He arrived at J7 because I used to train his mum, Joanne, in my council classes more than ten years ago.

DJ is such a wonderful, loving boy. His attitude is so positive. Every time he comes in, he'll take any opportunity he gets to give me a hug or challenge me to a dance-off. He mainly struggles with speech and expressing himself, but when it comes to training he is incredible. Training him is a dream because there is nothing he will say no to. Anything that I ask him to do, he'll give it a go, to the best of his ability, and that's all you can ask of anybody. His only setting is giving 110 per cent. He's a man after my own heart.

And he is *unbelievably* strong. The first time I saw his ability, I thought, *I'm going to expose as much amazing awesomeness from this kid as I can.* He'll do press-ups

YOU ARE NOT YOUR LIMITS

with a clap. He'll do burpees. He is admirably athletic, which is rarer for people with Down syndrome. He is incredibly energetic. He's got one of the greatest squats and squat jumps you'll ever see. He's like a kangaroo! We've done drills where I've had him landing one-legged pistol squats on top of boxes. How hard is it? Man, just Google it! DJ defies the odds. I'm constantly blown away by his athletic ability.

He boggles my mind on a weekly basis. One time, I had him standing between two stacks of weights that came up to his waist. I asked him to jump up high and land with one foot on top of each one. I'll tell you now, most fully able guys of his age would not have been able to even think of doing it.

DJ stood there, in his black Oasis t-shirt, and took a deep breath. The first time he jumped, he didn't quite make it. Nor the second. I gave him a little pep talk. 'I'll always treat you normal, but you're *not* normal!' I yelled. 'You're DJ. You're sensational!' He leapt in the air and landed on the stacks perfectly. Magnificent!

Another time, I stood DJ in front of a high bar and told him to squat jump over it from a standing start. The bar was right up to his chest. It looked impossible – but DJ does the impossible. 'Go on, DJ, attack it!' I said, and he leapt over the bar first time. I roared in delight as DJ pointed his finger in triumph at the camera filming him.

We even have our own catchphrase. Sometimes, when

IT TAKES A VILLAGE

I'm training DJ and we're filming it to put online, I'll encourage him by yelling, 'If anyone can, DJ can!' And, bro, I mean it. It's not just words. Believe you me, DJ is a superman.

*

DJ is a natural in the gym – he's strong, he gives it all he's got – and he took to it like a duck to water. But I knew, before I even opened J7, that it had to work for everyone. Like I say, when people are wary of exercising, a gym can be a lonely and scary place. Terrifying, really. A lot of women, and young blokes, and elderly people, and disabled people, can find gyms horrible places. They might go once and never go back. And that was the exact opposite of what I wanted J7 to be like.

All sorts came in, those first few weeks and months. People I knew from the council classes. Newcomers. Young. Old. People who trained every day; those who popped in once or twice a week. Just regular members of the local community. That was exactly what I wanted. The community I had dreamed of started to form in front of my eyes. But I still knew I had to keep an eye on things to make sure the atmosphere was exactly right. I needed to see the space from the viewpoint of someone who was unsure of themselves in a gym, not just from my point of view, as someone who has always loved sport and exercise and is totally comfortable in this kind of environment.

'The community I had dreamed of started to form in front of my eyes.'

IT TAKES A VILLAGE

After all, true communities can only be built when we think about and respect each other.

So, initially, I got a few hardcore bodybuilders in. The kind of guys whose torsos look like upside-down triangles, and who yell as they lift crazy amounts of weights. Now, I've nothing against those guys (I *am* one! I've taken up powerlifting in recent years). I fully respect them and what they do. I meant what I said: I wanted the space to be welcoming to *everyone*. But for that to work, everyone needed to turn up with a certain attitude. J7 wasn't a place for ego.

What if my mum came in, or Brenda, or one of my elderly or disabled clients, and there were enormous blokes with their shirts off, sweating, and shouting, and smashing heavy weights off the floor? It would freak them out. It would frighten them. And I wasn't having that.

So, in the first weeks, I had to take a few bodybuilders to one side and say, 'Sorry, mate, you can't take your vest off in here. You can't grunt and scream as you lift. We're not that sort of gym.' They didn't kick off at me because I was very polite and respectful in the way I explained it to them. They understood. They just didn't come back.

Everyone has an equal right to train and get healthy. It doesn't matter if they've been training for ten years or ten minutes. The person who has just picked up a 2kg dumbbell for the first time is as important as the person who knows all the theory and can lift heavy.

YOU ARE NOT YOUR LIMITS

If someone is nervous of the gym, I only get one opportunity to persuade them to start training. Only one opportunity to show them just how amazing exercise can be. If they get scared, or I scare them off, they might never come back. So, I have to get it right, from the very start.

I put so much thought into the atmosphere because I wanted people, as soon as they walked into the centre, to think: *I belong here.* A big part of that is music. There's always music playing and it's not just generic stuff. I don't just stick on Kiss FM, or Heart Radio. I'll sometimes put on bespoke tunes, according to who is coming in.

In the early days, a beautiful elderly Irish lady who I called Aunty Veronica used to train with us. Sadly, she's passed away now, but when she was in, I used to play an Irish jig called 'I'll Tell Me Ma': 'I'll tell me ma, when I get home, the boys won't leave the girls alone.' She loved it because it reminded her of growing up in Ireland.

There is another older, Jamaican lady I call Aunty Gloria, and I play her an old Bob Marley song to take her back to her days in Kingston. I play Elvis for another older lady who remembers dancing to his tunes as a girl in clubs on Portobello Road in London. I put a lot of effort into choosing the right music because it helped to create a vibe that made them feel at home. So often there is an attitude that we must bend ourselves to fit to the gym, but I think these spaces can adapt so they fit their clients.

Once my disabled clients started to find me, a lot of the

IT TAKES A VILLAGE

younger ones came with carers and parents. So, I wanted the space to feel good for them, too. If you love someone and see them face challenges every day, you are probably going to feel quite protective of them. So, that's even more people who have to feel welcome, who need to know that our space is for everyone, even if they are not the ones who will be working out. Though I get a few involved too, even when they are not expecting to do any exercise themselves, don't you worry!

DJ is a lucky young man because he has a fantastic dad, Dean, and a mum who adores him and who will do anything for him. I am lucky enough to have a brilliant family myself and I know how much they have influenced who I am as a person. My brother, Tyrone, and I have two beautiful parents who've always protected us and cared for us. My mum and dad, Audrey and Clyde McLean, are the most loving people. A lot of what I am now comes from having parents who love me and who've never been afraid to show me that love. And this is something I see all the time at J7 – a lot of love from parents who really want to encourage their kids.

I was born in Spanish Town, Jamaica, which is one of the rougher areas – and I came to the UK when I was five. My family had to work hard to survive. I was too little to really appreciate all that was going on, but now that I'm older, I understand the sacrifices my family made to get by and look after me.

YOU ARE NOT YOUR LIMITS

When I was growing up, my dad worked in a restaurant in a fancy hotel called The Midland. Dad's so polite and well-mannered that he got on great there. Even now, he talks about how much he loved that job: 'Ah, let me tell you, when I was at The Midlands . . .' (as he always calls it, lol!). A lot of my morals and principles have come from my father. He's taught me about hard work and sacrifice, and I try to follow his example, now that I'm a grown man with a wife and two sons of my own.

What can I say about my mum? She's the most giving person in the world. All she's ever wanted is to make sure Tyrone and I are OK. She's instilled a drive in me: try to improve every day. She's always told me: 'There are so many things out there for you to go and get. So, go and get them!' She's been like that since I was born.

I'm a mini-me of my mum, with the same attitude and stubbornness. That means we butt heads all the time. We can argue and not talk to each other for two weeks. We'll blank each other in the street. But then we'll look at each other, laugh and be back to normal. She's a wonderful woman. I love Mum to bits.

Every child wants their parent's love and approval. Whenever Mason or Leo is trying to do something, I'm watching them with interest and with excitement. We live in a world where, for all sorts of reasons, lots of children – no matter what their state of health or what they can or can't do – don't get the parenting they deserve. I wish it

IT TAKES A VILLAGE

were different. Particularly when I see with my own eyes, day in, day out, how much love and joy there is in families like DJ's.

I'm in no position to judge, but I have to say how full of admiration I am for Joanne and for Dean, and the way they can meet their situation.

JOANNE:

When we first went to J7, I said that I hoped that Javeno would be able to push DJ. Well, I didn't have to worry on that score! When he saw that DJ was super-keen and wanted to do well, he started to really challenge him every week. And DJ welcomes that. It's exactly what he wants.

Javeno has had him flipping huge tractor tyres over. He's had him jumping over chairs. Dragging massive weights around the car park. Lifting heavier and heavier bars. DJ adores it, especially when he's got Javeno in his ear, shouting, 'If anyone can, DJ can!'

DJ loves nothing more than doing his best. We go to J7 every Wednesday, and as soon as we leave, DJ starts his countdown to the next Wednesday. Every morning, he tells me how many days there are to go. If he could go there every day, he would.

We'll go to J7, and Javeno will ask, 'What do you want to do today, DJ? Because you're so good, you can do anything you want!' It's just what he needs to hear. Some weeks, they lace the gloves up and Javeno gives him a boxing lesson. Once, DJ thumped Javeno in his privates by mistake. He certainly felt it!

Javeno makes him smile. He treats him like he treats everybody else, and that's all I've ever wanted for him. Javeno doesn't care that he's got Down syndrome. He makes him feel like he's his mate. Well, he is his mate.

DJ has his happiest times in J7. I honestly don't know how Javeno dreams up some of the wild and wacky things that he has him doing. And you can see he really cares.

Every morning, DJ and I look at Javeno's social media to see what he's put up. DJ loves it when he's on there. He really wants to go on the telly. We went to Asda one day, and a guy ran up and started talking to DJ.

'I've seen you on Instagram!' he said.

'Yeah,' said DJ.

'You're amazing!' the guy told him.

'Do you want my autograph?' DJ asked. Honestly, he laps it up.

Javeno did a podcast with Tyson Fury's company. He messaged me to watch it. We did, and Javeno had set up a picture of DJ, in a photo frame, right next to the host as they talked.

6.
YOU ARE SEEN

AIMEE:

I've always had major medical issues. My mum had me very early, when she was only 29 weeks pregnant. Because I couldn't breathe, I was on life support at first, then in an incubator for six weeks. I had to be fed through a tube for the first six months of my life and I've had two major bleeds to the brain.

I got diagnosed with cerebral palsy at 18 months and I've been in a wheelchair ever since. I was in a mainstream primary school, then I was moved to a special needs high school, but I really wanted to stay mainstream. My mum fought hard for me and managed to get me transferred after 18 months.

I'm mentally quite an 'up' person, but growing up with cerebral palsy hasn't been easy. A lot of sufferers struggle with their words and what they want to say. I feel grateful that I'm able to express myself, but I've had to work really hard to get to the point I'm at now.

As a kid, I was given physio sessions and I worked really hard in them. But that all goes out of the window when you hit 16. The physio can stop as funding changes. That seems wrong to me: unfortunately, cerebral palsy is a lifetime thing, so the physio should be constant. Because without physio . . . well, if you don't use it, you lose it.

School was OK but I've never really been an academic person. I think I'm more of a people person. My big passion has always been music and singing. My favourite artist is Ariana Grande. I'm a massive, massive fan of everything that she's done.

My mum took me to see Ariana Grande at the Manchester Arena in May 2017, when I was 18. It was the concert that was attacked by a suicide bomber, when 22 people were killed. My mum had just pushed me into a lift when the bomb went off, after the concert. I was half a second from being hit by the blast. It's a miracle that I'm still alive, really.

I saw loads of shrapnel go flying past. Bolts and bits of metal. It was a very out-of-body experience. People were lying dead and injured on the floor, including very young kids. Everyone was screaming

YOU ARE SEEN

and there was blood everywhere. My mum worked in intensive care at the time, and I said to her that she should go and try and save people.

My mum looked at me and asked, 'What if there's another explosion?' I said, 'Look, that girl lying there looks about eight! I've had 18 years of my life. If another bomb goes off, it goes off. Please go and help her!' Mum ran over to her. I think she probably did save lives that day.

The bomb squad came to our house later to ask questions. They said, 'We've seen you on the CCTV. We genuinely don't know how you survived.' It's ironic, really. Some people assume I'm in a wheelchair because of the attack. But it's actually because I was in a wheelchair, and had to be pushed into a lift, that I'm still here.

It was a horrible experience. I wouldn't wish it on my worst enemy. It's something that I don't think you ever get over. You just learn to live with it. The night sweats kicked in really bad. I had two rounds of trauma therapy. They wanted me to have more but I said, 'There's only so many times you can go over one thing.'

After the bombing, I got diagnosed with depression and PTSD. I've always had anxiety, but I'm the sort of person who doesn't want to admit it. Nobody wants to admit they've got mental health issues. But at that point, I had no choice. I was so low that I didn't see an out. And I really, really wanted to find an out.

And then I found Javeno.

A friend sent me one of Javeno's videos, filmed at the health centre. I watched it and thought, *I need to get in touch with this guy.* My friend managed to get hold of his number and contacted him on my behalf. Then Javeno rang me. Which was another very out-of-body experience.

Javeno asked, 'Where are you from?'

'I'm from Stockport, Greater Manchester,' I said. And he put the phone down on me.

I thought, huh? What's going on? I rang him back. Javeno answered and said, 'I don't want to hear from you – I want to see you! Get down to J7 now!'

I went to meet him and it immediately felt like I'd known him for ten years. The first thing he did was hug me, the same way I'd seen him online hugging his other clients. It was weird at first, to see him in person after seeing him online, but it felt so great. And, from that day, he became the best friend I never knew I needed.

It was September 2022 when I met Javeno. Ever since then, we've been inseparable. He doesn't see your disability and he never has. Regardless of whether you're in a wheelchair, he classes you as

YOU ARE SEEN

a normal person and tells you that you are there to work. That's what I love about Javeno.

*

After my pep talk from Tyrone during Covid, I decided to take social media more seriously. I started to post a lot more on Instagram and Facebook. But that doesn't mean that I spent loads of time carefully crafting epic Hollywood movies. Because I've never done that. I hate the *fakeness* you get in so much social media. You look at some people's feeds and they're so scripted. They've spent ages trying to make it all look perfect, but it just looks corny. Well, I can't be doing with that.

The way I do social media is very, very basic. I ask someone if they're OK with me filming them. If they are, I point a phone at them or, usually, one of my team does, and we shoot a minute or two. We press record. Press stop. Press send. That's it. End of story. No edits. No tweaks. I'm an exercise specialist, not Steven Spielberg!

We started doing it more as soon as we reopened after Covid. And a mad, unexpected, brilliant thing happened. If anybody had predicted it, I'd have thought they were a total weirdo: *'Bro! What have you been smoking?'* And, if I'm honest with you, I still can't believe it.

In a very short time, hundreds of people began following us. Then it was thousands. Then, hundreds of thousands. And, suddenly, my cool disabled guys, training their hearts out every week in my little orange gym in Old Market Street, Blackley, were impressing millions of people. Yes, *millions*. And I don't just mean in Britain! We'd film a vid, put it up, and within minutes, or even seconds, we'd get comments – lovely, positive, appreciative comments – from Germany, America, Australia, Brazil, Japan, South Africa... you name it! J7 went – what do the kids call it? – *viral*.

Well, that Tyrone, eh? He knows his shit!

How did I feel when it first happened? Bloody surprised! But when the shock died down and I got my head around it, I was delighted because I realised that it would be great for the guys I trained. It would make them feel seen. Appreciated.

When Aimee – or any of the others who get involved in social media – comes to the gym and does a great session, I can see that this work creates happiness. And the amazing, brilliant, fantastic thing is that nowadays, it's not just me who sees that joy. It goes right around the world. Because the internet has taken J7 global.

It's one of the best things that's ever happened to J7. It's taken guys who are used to being made to feel invisible, or inferior, because of their disabilities, and it's given them an audience and a platform. It's turned them into role models, heroes – and it inspires me to keep going and reach more people. But most of all, it does what I can't do.

I never sugarcoat things for Josh or Aimee or Kiera. I'll never tell them, 'Oh, you're doing great!' if they're

YOU ARE SEEN

slacking and not progressing. But those guys are normally busting a gut in J7, so I can say, 'That's fantastic! You're doing really well! Getting so much better!' But do they always take it in? No. I reckon sometimes they think, *oh, it's just Javeno saying that. He has to because it's his job to look out for us and encourage us. He's just being our big bro.* But when they read other people, *strangers*, from all across the world saying beautiful things about them – well, that's different!

Josh or Aimee will come into the gym and say, 'J, look at the amazing things this person in Australia has said about me on TikTok! They say that I'm strong, and I'm beautiful, and they've been watching me improve so much!' And I laugh, and I say, "I've been telling you that for *weeks*, you muppets!"'

And I have. But when I've said it, although we love each other, they might have thought, *oh, it's just Jav. Whatevs.* It can go in one ear and out the other. But when it's a person, or rather thousands of people, from outside the 'family' saying it to them, it hits home. And it lifts them up.

While we're training, though, even if we decide to make a little film, we don't get distracted by social media. I love that these guys have discovered their power to help and inspire people they have never met, that's incredible beyond words, but we still make sure that when they are at the gym, it's just about them – their progress, their ability and their *fun*.

YOU ARE NOT YOUR LIMITS

When I was in India, I had one of those moments when, by chance, I heard a saying that immediately spoke to me. It's a thing that occasionally happens in life. You're going about your day as usual, and you hear or read something that resonates. For me, that phrase was *the ministry of presence*. And I've tried my hardest to live by it ever since.

It describes being present in the moment, all the time. Focused, and sharp, and intense. More specifically, it means giving the person I'm with, whether I'm just chatting to them or training them, my full focus and attention. Making sure that it's all about them. That *I'm* all about them.

When I'm training Aimee, or anyone else, I home in on them 100 per cent. I look closely at everything they do and I listen to every word they say. For the length of the session, I want them to be fully aware that I'm there for them and them alone.

I make eye contact. Too many people overlook wheelchair users – literally! They don't even bother to look down, or get on their level, to talk to them. Addressing someone properly when you're talking to them is not only respectful, but it also builds closeness and trust. It builds friendship.

While I'm training with someone in the centre, nothing in the world will come between us. For those 30 minutes, anybody else who turns up in the gym is irrelevant. It could be people coming for business meetings with me.

YOU ARE SEEN

It could be the King of England, Erling Haaland or Beyoncé. It wouldn't matter who it was. They just have to wait.

Camera crews have come to J7 to film for the local news. When they arrive, I tell them: 'No disrespect, but you guys are irrelevant. If you're watching us work, just film. Record and stay out of the way. Don't get involved. The most important thing here – no, the *only* important thing – is the person I'm training.'

If I give the disabled guys I train in my gym my total attention, encouragement and love, it can make a massive difference. It can influence their lives in a monumental, positive way. That's what I've ended up dedicating my life to doing. It's the reason I wanted to create a space where people can come and be both strong and vulnerable, while always knowing they are safe and supported.

That's the ministry of presence. It's giving disabled people the respect and the appreciation they deserve. Everybody needs to be appreciated. And the great thing now is that I appreciate Aimee when she's in J7 – and when she goes home, and she looks at her phone, thousands of people all over the world are appreciating her as well. *Result!*

Obviously, none of my disabled clients at J7 have had an easy life, but Aimee has had it harder than most. Not only was she born with cerebral palsy, but she also survived a terrible incident a few years ago. Yet somehow, through it all, she manages to stay ridiculously happy and positive.

YOU ARE NOT YOUR LIMITS

Let me tell you, no bigger superstar has ever come through my door than Aimee.

When I first met Aimee, my big thing was trying to do what I could so she didn't get influenced too negatively by the world we're living in, because of the awful stuff she'd experienced at the Ariana Grande concert. It's understandable for a young girl to go through something like that and develop a harrowing world view. I wanted to get across to Aimee that yeah, OK, there are bad things and bad people out there, but the world is still a good place. A wonderful place. But it was so much easier than I thought it would be, because Aimee is one of the most brilliant, positive people in the world.

She is very similar to Josh in that she loves being lifted out of her chair. It feels like freedom, she says. This is something that able-bodied people will never fully understand because we're not permanent wheelchair users. We take for granted a thing that, for Josh or Aimee or any other paraplegic person, feels miraculous.

When I get Aimee out of her chair and we're training, I challenge her hard. If I don't, I'm just putting her in a box and that's what society has done to her already. It's put her in a box and said, 'You're a wheelchair user, and that is what defines you.' And that's the exact opposite of what the training should be about.

For anybody, able or disabled, to keep developing, they have to be challenged. We have to fail at things in order to

YOU ARE SEEN

say, 'OK, let's go again and give it another try.' That's what we do: fail, repeat, achieve; fail, repeat, achieve. I've even got those words on my orange walls. Forget able. Forget disabled. Every *human* needs those challenges.

So, I lift Aimee out of her wheelchair. And the great thing is that, when I do, she's bloody hilarious. I will have her on the floor doing something and, without thinking, I might say, 'OK, just stay there, I'll be back in a second.' And she'll look at me and say, 'I've got to bloody stay here! My legs don't work!'

What have been my favourite sessions with Aimee? I hardly know where to start! I'll never forget the time I helped her out of her chair, laid her on her tummy and told her to hit a ball into a goal two metres away with a tiny toy golf stick. It was a great workout for her coordination – and sounds pretty easy, right? Wrong!

Aimee kept thwacking that ball and it kept rolling wide of the goal. *Thwack.* Wide. *Thwack.* Wide. I gave her some encouraging words: 'Come on!' We could hardly speak for laughing. On about her tenth go, she managed it. *Yeeesss!* In typical Aimee fashion, she wrote on Instagram: 'It's harder than it looks because the floor is slanted.'

I love sessions where we play games and have a laugh, but I also want to help my clients practise for potential real-life scenarios. Like with Kiera and the hoovering. Once, I laid Aimee on her back on a mat, flipped her wheelchair over, and asked her to imagine that she'd fallen out of her chair in the middle of nowhere, and had to get help. The only way for her to do that was to reach a phone that I'd put on a chair about ten feet away and make a call to get some assistance.

Aimee managed to wriggle forward on her back then rolled onto her front. 'Go on! Get that phone!' I encouraged. She used her elbows to inch forward. She had to stop once to catch her breath, but she moved up to the chair and got the phone. *Wow!* I whooped so loud that I almost deafened her.

Aimee is a ball of joy. And I'm in awe every time I see her. I've got a loud voice and the gift of the gab, but words fail me a little bit when it comes to describing Aimee. She is literally one of the sweetest people I've ever met, or that anybody could ever meet.

AIMEE:

Javeno is absolutely bonkers. I cannot explain how bonkers he is. From the moment you get there, he's always doing something wacky. He's doing weird little dances or telling dad jokes which he thinks are funny but aren't funny at all. They're actually really, really cringe.

I never wanted anyone to mollycoddle me. Just because someone's got a disability doesn't mean they can't achieve the things they want to achieve. Javeno judges it so well. He doesn't push people beyond

YOU ARE SEEN

their limits, but he pushes them to the point that he knows they can get to.

With me, he knows he can try anything and I'll give it my best shot. He throws me in at the deep end and I love it. I always put 100 per cent into his sessions because, let's not forget, he does it all for free.

Every time I go to J7, Javeno helps me out of my wheelchair, and it's wonderful. It's one of my favourite things. It makes me feel more . . . free. It may sound weird but, for that short time while I'm out, I feel liberated.

Sometimes, Javeno will be training me and he'll tell me, 'Stay there, don't move!' And I'll laugh and say, 'Where exactly do you think I'm going to go?' Or he'll explain something to me and then ask, 'Do you understand?' And I'll answer, 'Of course I do! I'm disabled, not stupid!' And we'll both be laughing our heads off.

We both give as good as we get. Too many people see my wheelchair and tiptoe around me. They think, oh, I shouldn't do or say anything out of line, in case I upset her. And I don't want that! I want people to talk to me just like they'd talk to anyone else. And that's what Javeno does.

If you look at his Instagram, and his TikTok, you see him telling me to 'make a poo noise' while I'm training! Well, cerebral palsy affects your tummy

'It may sound weird but, for that short time while I'm out, I feel liberated.'

YOU ARE SEEN

muscles, so it can take me a while to go to the toilet. So when Javeno asks me to make a poo noise, it could be dangerous! Javeno is doing what he always does: taking a bad situation and turning it into a joke. Into a laugh. Turning it into joy.

Believe it or not, at the time of writing, I've got nearly 20,000 followers on TikTok. Nearly 20,000! It's an amazing number of people and it just keeps growing. They all love watching my progress and they all love seeing how invigorated it makes me feel.

When I was growing up, I never had anybody outside my family looking out for me and telling me that everything was going to be alright. Then I met Javeno. He does that, and I want to do it for people younger than me, who are in a similar situation. I want to tell them that everything is going to be alright.

I get messages from people all over the world telling me that I help them get out of bed in the morning, and I give them a reason to carry on. I'll never get used to that. It's the best feeling in the world, because all I've ever wanted to do is inspire and help people like me. And now I can do it.

I post Javeno's videos from J7 on my feed as well and I get hundreds and hundreds of messages in reply. I read them all. Someone messaged me recently and said he'd been watching Javeno's videos of Kiera,

Josh, Fran and me, and they've been a big help to him. The guy said he has a feeding tube and he used to be really embarrassed about it. But now he's seen us, and the strength we all show, he's realised that having a feeding tube isn't such a bad thing. We've helped him cope and get stronger in himself.

I was on TikTok live when I read his message and I had to come offline because I was blubbing so much – with happiness! I felt like I couldn't breathe for joy. I messaged the guy back immediately and said how happy I was and how proud of him I felt. Honestly, getting messages like that means more to me than I can ever begin to explain.

I couldn't care less about getting well-known or being recognised. It's about knowing that other disabled people are getting something out of what I do.

I've made so much physical progress since I started going to J7. A week ago, I actually managed to take my shirt off on my own. That's a massive achievement for me. Unlike my physios, Javeno tells me: 'Aimee, you can do whatever you want to do.' And I've started to believe him. To believe in myself.

7.
CHANNEL YOUR INNER DOG

SARAH:

Noah is autistic and has cerebral palsy. I was only 25 weeks pregnant when I gave birth to him. Because he was so early, the doctors said he might not walk and he might not talk. In fact, they said he might not live.

Noah's had chronic lung disease; he's had a grade two bleed on the brain; he's had heart surgery. He couldn't walk until a week before his third birthday, and he couldn't talk until he was in reception at school. He's had so many complications and hurdles in his little life already, and yet, somehow, he gets through them all and keeps going.

He's an amazing guy, a lovely little boy, always eager to try things. He bounces around all day, smiling, and never lets anything stop him. Even if he's in pain or he's struggling with something, he stays cheerful. He just gets on with everything the best that he can.

When Noah was six, he had to have muscle-lengthening surgery in his left leg. We didn't really want to do it, because he was so young, but his foot was in such a bad position that he couldn't even get his shoes on. He has to wear two splints on his legs every day, to keep his legs straight, and night splints as well.

The day after the leg surgery, the physios came and got him up and walking with a little Zimmer frame. As his mum, I could see Noah was in pain, even though he only said, 'Oh, it hurts!' once. But he didn't cry; he never cries. He just kept moving, and doing what they asked him to, with a little smile on his face.

A few weeks later, I took him to a christening. They had bouncy castles and all the other kids were jumping around, but Noah was really struggling. He was just sat on his own and then he asked me if we could go home. And I thought, I didn't put him through surgery for this! I need to take him to Javeno!

I'd discovered Javeno around 2019, when he popped up on my Instagram, and I started following him. It had dawned on me that I wanted him to work with Noah. Noah is a big boy but not very mobile and I wanted a physio to get him moving. I was like, how do I get hold of this guy?

I wrote him an Instagram message but I thought, nah, I bet he gets loads of people doing that. So, in the end, I just went to J7 with Noah. Noah didn't want to go. He's had physio before and always hated it because it's usually very serious and functional. So, when I said we were going to see a trainer called Javeno, he was, like, 'No! No! No!'

J7 is right on the other side of Manchester but we drove over anyway. It was a Friday evening. Javeno was so welcoming to both of us. He said to me, 'Can I ask you why you want me to work with your son?' I said, 'He needs help. I'm not a physio. I do what I can for him, but he needs more.' And then Javeno started chatting to Noah.

Due to his autism, Noah doesn't always comprehend what's said to him. Javeno asked him, 'Where are you from?'

Noah answered, 'I don't know.'

'OK, where is your dad from?' asked Javeno.

'Jamaica,' said Noah.

'I knew you were Jamaican!' Javeno shouted. 'I'm Jamaican as well! Let's stick together!'

Javeno was laughing his head off and Noah started laughing as well. Noah instantly took a real shine to

YOU ARE NOT YOUR LIMITS

him. He loved him straight away. It was almost like he sensed that this man was going to be good for him.

People sometimes ask me, both in real life and on social media, how I'm always so *up*. So cheerful. They'll say, 'How do you *do* it, man? Don't you ever wake up at 5 a.m., on a grey Manchester morning, a bit weary and shitty, and feel like saying, "Fuck it, I can't be bothered today?"'

And what's my answer? *'NO!'* I mean, of course I have days when I'm down, outside of work. Everyone has days like that sometimes, and I'm no different. But when it comes to what I get to do every day, and the special, special guys that I train – no way! It would just never happen. How could I ever feel down, or jaded, around my superstars?

I'm constantly in awe of them. I've said it before, and I'll say it again: things that we take for granted are luxuries for them. We don't have to think, and work hard, just to turn our heads. To scratch our ears. They perform miracles every day. So, I'd be a pretty selfish man if I ever woke up and thought, *nah, I can't be arsed today!*

Also, another thing that I have become aware of, since I started working with more people with different disabilities, is how disabled people are often used to a certain pattern of abandonment. They're used to people saying they're difficult or hard to work with. But for them to relax, to start to believe in the idea that they can be part of the J7 community, they need to know that isn't something that's going to happen here.

With some people, I tackle this head-on. I did it with Josh right at the beginning and it's something I've carried on doing. All the issues that might have been in his mind, I brought them right to the front of the conversation and I destroyed them. When I first meet someone, I say, 'Look, if you do come here, I'm not going to abandon you. I won't find you difficult or hard work. There is no end date to us working together.' I tell my disabled clients this from day one because I know that in so many cases this is not what they're used to. They're used to being in hospital, or at a rehab centre, where they get given a four-week physio programme, or six weeks, and then it's done. Over. Finished. So I let them know immediately that J7 isn't like that.

'I'll train you and I'll be with you as long as you're willing to be here,' I say. And, for me, the other important thing is to let them know that the feeling is reciprocal. They have gone to the effort of choosing to come to J7, to let me train them, and I have chosen *them*, as well, and I always will. Society might sometimes look elsewhere and pick other people to put up on a pedestal, but it's crucial that my guys know that I've chosen them, and I'm not going anywhere.

Nobody is ever going to make them feel that they are inferior, or invisible, or they shouldn't be here. Because they *belong* here. I want to make sure they know that this is how it works at J7. Nobody likes feeling like a nuisance, do they? No one wants to feel like a bother. A lot of disabled people, when they go to gyms, will worry: *oh, no! Somebody will have to open the door for me! I'll be in the way! A burden!* I make it clear that that sort of thing will never, never happen in the J7 community.

This is the attitude shared by everyone who works at J7. As I've got busier, I can't be in the gym 24/7 like I used to anymore, but, thankfully, we now have a really established, fantastic team, so people can still come in and train with someone, even when I am not there. If I have to miss a session, I make sure that I always catch up with whoever it is the next time – that they not only know that I miss their company, but they never, ever think I'm abandoning them.

Finding the right staff isn't nearly as straightforward as it would be for your average gym, though! I want everyone to feel comfortable at J7, regardless of who they train with. Everyone who comes here needs to know the wins they make are down to them and don't belong to me or any other person. Yeah, I like to think I am good at my job, but it's the individual's hard work that makes the magic happen!

An ideal trainer for J7 is obviously not the person with the biggest biceps, the best six-pack or the most training certificates. It's the one with the biggest heart.

CHANNEL YOUR INNER DOG

It's somebody who is willing to really connect with people, able or disabled, young or old, on a spiritual and personal level, and to do it day in, day out.

Training has to be done with care and love. It can't be flashy or gimmicky or it just won't work. I don't care what my staff look like. I don't care how much they can bench press or how much they can deadlift. I care that they *get* what we're doing at J7, and they engage with it on a very deep level. As a gym trainer, you're supposed to encourage people. You're meant to say 'Yay!' and congratulate them. But not in a superficial, pretend way, with a fake Hollywood smile and gleaming teeth. Because people, disabled or otherwise, will see right through that. You have to be fully invested in them, and you have to mean it.

I've never actively advertised for trainers – the right ones have found their way here naturally. Like almost everything that's come about here, it's tended to be a happy accident. My main right-hand man at J7 is a guy called Badger. Well, his mother didn't name him that when he was born! She called him James. But I call him Badger because, well, he looks like a badger. Badger joined one of my exercise classes nearly ten years ago, well before I opened J7. He wasn't a PT instructor. He was doing different jobs back then: working in cafes and in offices. But he was the nicest person and I could see that his heart was so big. And, one day, I just told him, 'You'd be brilliant working with me.'

YOU ARE NOT YOUR LIMITS

Badger had never thought about a career as a trainer but I didn't need to convince him. He loved the idea from the get-go. And, as soon as he started training people, I saw how much they loved him. I told him, 'Mate, you can change so many people's lives!' And he has. Because there's nothing fake about him.

There are a lot of gym trainers out there who fake it. They pretend to be interested and involved in clients' lives when they're not. They pretend that you're doing great, and you've lost so much weight, or they say, 'Wow! Look how much muscle you've gained!' But training should be so much more than a physical change. And they're probably just feeling the pressure to make money in this economy.

Badger isn't like that. He treats everyone the same and he builds rock-solid relationships with them. He's joined this journey, this thing that I've created, and embodied it as if it was his own. Which it *is*, now. He understands that the secret of J7 is creating a vibe, an atmosphere, where people feel at home.

I'd never force Badger to work as hard as I do. I'd never ask him to match my crazy 90-hour working week. But he has a great work ethic and he goes above and beyond the call of duty on a daily basis. He has incredible commitment, and I'm very grateful to him for that.

Just as I'm constantly grateful to all the elite humans who have chosen me to be part of their story and to train them – from a 60-year-old warrior like Paul to a brave, funny eight-year-old boy like Noah, who is brought to the centre by his mum, Sarah.

*

I loved Noah the second I set eyes on him. When I saw him, I just saw my son. Noah is the same age as Mason, and he's got the same beautiful mixed-race complexion, the same brown eyes, the same smile. The same pure innocence. I couldn't wait to work with him and help him to do amazing things.

I remember, in our very first session together, I was explaining to Noah that exercise is not about muscles, or how quick you can run, or how high you can jump. It's about the amazing feeling you can get from doing it.

Noah's got two leg splints on but he doesn't take them off when he's training. He just cracks on. His resilience is so inspiring. He doesn't hesitate. He just does whatever we need to do. We do a lot of leg work. I get him to sit down and look in the mirror and see how high he can raise them. He might struggle sometimes, but we always find a way to get it done.

I don't care about Noah's skill level in our sessions. Obviously, there's an element of skill to doing certain things but, really, his skill level is irrelevant. It's about work ethic. Work rate. Intensity. That's what counts and, luckily, Noah has a really strong work ethic. This means that exercise gives him an amazing feeling he can take beyond the training.

One time I asked him to lift a medicine ball up to his chest. He picked it up off the floor and got it as high as his tummy but then had to put it down. He was finding it tricky so I gave him a pep talk. 'Go on, Noah!' I said. 'Channel your inner superhero! Or channel your inner... what's your favourite animal?'

Noah thought hard. 'A dog,' he said.

'OK,' I laughed. 'Channel your inner dog!' Noah bent down again but fell over the ball onto his hands and knees. He used all his might to lift that ball off the floor and up to his chest. He channelled his inner dog.

Another time, I got him stepping up and down onto platforms that I kept making higher. We alternated leading with his stronger leg and weaker leg. It was tough for Noah, but he was so proud of what he was achieving: 'Mum! Look!'

When he got onto the last, highest step, I cheered like a crazy man and gave him a bear hug. He deserved it.

Noah comes from a wonderful family. His mum, Sarah, is so loving and caring and completely adores him.

But it's important to talk directly to him. *Communicate.* Often people will ignore a disabled child and talk to their parent instead: 'Is he OK?' 'Does he need anything?' 'Does he want a drink?' To which the parent will say: 'Ask him!'

CHANNEL YOUR INNER DOG

Noah does talk to me but I have trained a few non-verbal people at J7, including the lovely Shania, who can say more with her eyes than most able kids can with their mouths. A lot of non-verbal children are like that. I remember meeting a wonderful little non-verbal girl called Holly a couple of years ago, at a disabled event in London.

Somebody connected to the event introduced me to Holly and her mum. He pointed at Holly. 'She loves my trainers!' he said.

So I looked at her and smiled. 'Oh, yeah?' I asked her. 'What's so good about his trainers? What's wrong with *mine*?'

I homed in on Holly and started talking to her. I was aware she was non-verbal, but I still wanted to treat her like any human being. She could understand. She wasn't stupid. I looked Holly in the face and talked to her for a while before I walked off.

Her mum called me back. She was really emotional. She said, 'I don't think you realise what you just did.'

'What did I do?' I asked.

'You talked to Holly. *Directly*. So many people don't. They talk through me: "Can you tell her this? Can you ask her to do that?"'

I hadn't even done it consciously. It had felt completely natural. While I was chatting to Holly, I had tunnel vision. I wasn't talking to 'a young girl who is non-verbal', or who has disability issue A, B, C or D. *I was talking to Holly.* Because if ever I can give a person love and attention, I am going to give it. And that's exactly what I do with Noah.

*

Noah can sometimes misinterpret something I say, often in a very literal way. He makes me laugh when he does that, but it's great. It's the innocence of Noah. And that innocence is a part of his magic.

Noah and I have some hilarious banter. One week, when I was training him, I told him that he was the world's strongest man. Ever since then, every time I ask him, 'Who is the world's strongest man, Noah?' he always says, 'Me! I am!' And I say, 'Yes, Noah, you *are* the world's strongest man. And the other strongest man is called Mitchell Hooper.'

Mitchell Hooper won the World's Strongest Man contest in 2023. He is a very kind, loving guy, and he happens to follow me on Instagram. He saw Noah telling me that he is the world's strongest man, and he sent Noah a beautiful message, encouraging him and bigging him up. It was unbelievable.

Training Noah is all about small victories. I take so much pride in every small victory that he achieves, and I celebrate them so much. Small victories have the potential to change someone's whole life. I always say you can't build a house without laying the first bricks. Noah is a

'Small victories have the potential to change someone's whole life.'

young man of eight years old, so we're building that house and laying those bricks down slowly. And I can't wait to see how he develops.

SARAH:

Noah loves going to J7 because Javeno pushes him and challenges him but he doesn't do it in a way that makes him struggle. He's so kind and nurturing with him. He finds ways to relate to Noah, connect with him, and banter. That's what makes it so fun and exciting for him.

I remember once he had Noah doing sit-ups. Noah used his hands to help, and Javeno laughed at him and said, 'No, you're cheating! That doesn't count!' Noah got back down, did them properly, and said, 'See!'

Javeno said, 'I knew you could do it, Noah!' And Noah loves it when he says things like that to him. His face was one big smile.

Another time, Javeno brought his son Mason in, and told Noah they were the Jamaican Olympic relay team. He had Noah running around the gym holding a baton, and he had rigged up a finish line from toilet paper. When Noah got to the line, he didn't know what to do and stopped in his tracks. Javeno had to rip the paper for him. It was very funny.

Going to J7 is the highlight of Noah's week.

CHANNEL YOUR INNER DOG

It's where he's happiest. I used to wonder if I'd have a problem getting him to go, once the novelty had worn off. But that hasn't happened. Because of his autism and his comprehension difficulties, you have to talk to Noah in a certain way. But Javeno is really good at doing it.

I couldn't believe it when Javeno called me and told me that Mitchell Hooper had put up a personal video message for Noah. Noah and I watched it together. Mitchell said, 'Noah, you are the world's strongest man, you can do anything, and I'm watching you!' Noah loved it.

8.
YOU ARE A LEADER

FRANCESCA:
It's been quite a difficult journey to get to be the young woman that I am now. But I have to be honest and say that, looking back, it's one that I'm proud of.

I was born with severe cerebral palsy and I've never been able to walk. I spent some time in special needs schools but was mainly in mainstream, which was a big thing for me. After school, until Covid came along, I worked as a receptionist and as a marketing assistant. It felt good to show society that disabled people can hold down a job.

In 2023, I was in hospital with anaemia and I had to have two blood transfusions. When I came out, I felt very down. I was hanging out at home one rainy day, with one of my support workers, and she said,

YOU ARE NOT YOUR LIMITS

'I want to show you this bloke on TikTok that you might like. He's wild and he's really funny.'

It was Javeno. I watched him and I thought, oh my goodness! This is something that I need! *I'd tried going to a gym once before, but I didn't like it. It felt like you had to be a certain way, and if you weren't, you didn't belong there. I wasn't comfortable there. But this . . . this was something else entirely.*

When I phoned the centre, Javeno answered. I was trying to be cool! I knew it was him by his voice, but I didn't want to come across as a super fangirl. But Javeno listened to me and said, 'Yeah, OK, come down.' I did. And, quite honestly, it's the best thing I've ever done.

When I met Javeno, he was exactly like he is on his videos. We hit it off right from the start, and I knew straight away that I could trust him and trust the process. I knew he had my back. And working with him has allowed me to . . . open up my voice.

Oh, my goodness! The things Javeno gets me doing! The great thing about him is that he loves exercise, but he's not on a quest to give us all the perfect abs, or the perfect core. It's so much more than that. He works with all of us on our mental health, too.

When I first went in, and he was getting me to move my feet, he asked me, 'Why are you coming here? Who are you doing it for?' I said that I was

YOU ARE A LEADER

doing it for my family and for myself but also, most importantly, for other people with cerebral palsy who don't have a voice or a champion. Because I'd like to be that voice and that champion.

Javeno made so much difference to me so quickly. After a few sessions, I noticed that my mentality had really shifted. I felt like I had started out on the best journey. My carer, Dawn, said to me, 'My God, you seem so different! You've got the biggest smile on your face!'

It was like I was having therapy that I didn't know I needed.

*

Why do I call myself 'a badass warrior with cerebral palsy'? Because I feel like I am! There are so many people with cerebral palsy who aren't lucky enough to have the platform that I have. I try to be a voice for them.

For me, it's the best job in the world to know that what I'm doing helps other people with cerebral palsy all over the world. I'm trying to advocate for them, and for their parents and carers, because they may feel that they don't belong in society. I'm trying to change that perspective and empower them.

I go into nurseries to try to educate really young children about disabilities and being in a wheelchair.

'I'd like to be that voice and that champion.'

YOU ARE A LEADER

Because those children grow up so quickly, and they start asking questions. And I don't want any disabled child to wonder, why can Mummy and Daddy walk, but I can't? *I don't want them thinking that they're any less. My mission has given me a purpose.*

It's easy for a lot of us to move through the world not seeing stuff, completely blinded by our own privilege. But there is a wonderfully sensitive, emotional, very caring young woman who is the exact opposite. Francesca is a true J7 superstar who reminds me, every time I see her, that the simplest things in life are the most amazing.

Fran has severe cerebral palsy but what she lacks in mobility, she makes up for in personality and character. She has an incredible presence. When she's in a room, she's heard and she's seen.

A lot of disabled and disadvantaged people question who they are and *what* they are at times. It's inevitable. Having to deal every day with a world that is often not set up for them means they can feel uncertain about their own existence and their own purpose. I think Fran felt like that at times. Though I genuinely think Fran was put on this planet to provoke amazing feelings in people. I've seen it with my own eyes so many times. She is fearless every time she comes to train, and then she goes home and inspires people all over the world. A lot of people make excuses in life, but Fran doesn't. She makes things happen.

YOU ARE NOT YOUR LIMITS

When you are feeling uncertain, you can often feel alone. And having good people around you at these times is so important. One of the many things that has come out of J7 that makes me very happy is that my disabled clients have all got to know each other. They've become close friends and that's one of the greatest things. J7 isn't just about them building a relationship with me. It's about opening the doors for them to also receive love, and form relationships, with other people.

It's a community. Fran, Josh, Aimee, Kiera, DJ and Tallulah all know and support each other. They all love each other. They have a WhatsApp group and they chat all the time. Because having a community is just as important as all the training and exercise we do together.

My love of team sports taught me early on about the energy and motivation you get when you come together to do something in a group, and this became even more obvious when I ran those big exercise classes that became almost like a party! But a few experiences at J7 have really shown me how important something else is. It's not just about community. It's also about getting the chance to be seen by, and connect to, others who have been through some of the same things. Though three of these opportunities sort of came about by accident.

I was training somebody when I suddenly had an idea. As I'm very spontaneous, I put up a post about it on my social media straight away: 'I want to set a world record,

YOU ARE A LEADER

guys. The biggest ever wheelchair exercise class. Who's interested?' And *Bang! Bang! Bang!* The response was insane. So, then I had to plan it and make it happen.

We did it just around the corner from J7, in June 2022, at the Abraham Moss Leisure Centre, where I used to take classes for the council. It turned into a bit of an event. Everybody really got into it, the local paper and local TV news came down, and it was a really joyous day. And we set a new record.

It went so well that I organised another attempt, at the same place, three months later. This time we did the biggest disabled exercise class, not just for wheelchair users, and we set a new world record again. We went back in March 2024 and we broke it again. This was just after I met Noah and Sarah, and they came along to watch and get involved.

All three occasions were great. The positive energy in the hall was something else. It was a lot of fun getting our photos taken with a big certificate in a frame. And having some press there, to show the world that of course disabled people can go to exercise classes *and* set records, was really good too. But what stands out for me most about those days were the connections I saw being made.

I remember, when we were setting the first world record, seeing a lady in a wheelchair who was a double amputee from the knees. I'd never met her before and I don't think I've seen her since. There was also a young girl there, probably nine or ten years old, who was exactly the same: another double amputee from the knees. The two of them saw each other, got deep in conversation, and were laughing and laughing. The little girl had never seen anybody with exactly the same condition before. She was literally staring at the lady's legs and saying, 'Oh, my God! Look!' It was a beautiful moment to see these two females, years apart in age but with exactly the same disability, getting on so well, talking about their condition and so happy to meet one another. And that was the wonderful thing about the world records. That was the message of the day. Not the numbers.

At the last world record, a lady from Bury who was a stroke survivor came along to join us. She'd seen some other stroke survivors on my social media so she came and sat with them. They were laughing, talking about their strokes, and comparing notes on rehabs and on recovery. Just making those shared, vital, human connections. It blew me away.

I saw people with Down syndrome talking to other people with Down syndrome. We had people with cerebral palsy, cancer, dementia, Parkinson's disease, all meeting people with the same conditions as them, sometimes for the first time, and having conversations and bonding. And that was the magic of the world-record days.

For what it's worth, if you *really* want to know, we had just over 80 people at the first record, more than 100 at the second, and over 120 at the third. But *who cares?*

YOU ARE A LEADER

Those days were about amazing, unique human beings turning up, meeting people who'd had the same experiences as them and encouraging each other.

*

When I can, I try to organise events for my superstars and community residents. In the past, we've held boxing nights to raise money for charity (we're raised more than £40,000 over the years). I put the gloves on to fight Queen Brenda – I tell everyone that she knocked me out!

It's not all about exercise, though. And nor is it just focused around disability and pushing the boundaries. Everyone, whoever they are, wants the chance to go out and enjoy themselves, right? In 2023, we got given some free tickets for Parklife Music Festival in Heaton Park in Manchester.

Yay! Let's have it! My superstars were well excited, especially Aimee and Fran, who are big music fans, and Kiera, who used to go to Parklife before she got ill. However, while it was an amazing festival, we had to cope with a lot of issues.

The promoters gave us passes for the disabled viewing platform. Nice! But it was totally open. There was no cover at all. And it was a roasting hot sunny day. When it gets too hot, able people can just get up and stroll to somewhere with some shade. But we couldn't do that. We were stuck in the blazing sun.

YOU ARE NOT YOUR LIMITS

My guys were really suffering and I was worried about them. I decided we had to get out of there. I was literally five minutes from taking them home when – guess what? – clouds came over, the heavens opened and we all got soaked. For once, we were glad of some Manchester rain!

The toilets were a huge problem. The only disabled toilets were right on the other side of the festival site. That meant having to wheel my guys through tens of thousands of drinking, partying people. And, when we got there, Josh's wheelchair was too big to fit in. The door wouldn't shut.

The festival organisers thought they were doing everything right, but they needed to take a much deeper look at the issue. They needed to think outside the box. Really, it's about getting educated in people's needs, and understanding what's required when it comes to disability access. Unparalleled amounts of organisational and logistical prep go into these kinds of events. The same amount of time and care needs to be spent on accessibility.

But credit where it's due. I spoke to the Parklife promoters afterwards and we had meetings. They apologised and promised to sort their stuff out.

I genuinely believe that all able-bodied people should experience being in a wheelchair for a few days. It would open their eyes. It would make them a lot more aware and considerate. It definitely helped me when I got injured and had to use a wheelchair for just a couple of weeks –

YOU ARE A LEADER

I'll tell you about that in a minute! In fact, I'm thinking of setting up a charity basketball or netball match. It would be a team of wheelchair users against a team of able people in wheelchairs.

*

From the outside, you might think that Fran's limited mobility might make it hard to train together. Well, I disagree. *You are not your limits.* I look at Fran and I see a million things that we can do. As long as there is movement, be it a turn, a lift, a wriggle, a twitch, we can work together. And I will encourage her to keep on moving.

When Fran first started coming to J7, we started off with some basic movements. I'd try to get her to move her feet, which she finds difficult. I'd get her to move her hands, which she finds *extremely* difficult.

But she did it – of course she did! She's a warrior. Then we could move on to some other things.

For example, there's another drill that I sometimes do with Fran, where I get her to pop a balloon full of water on my head. It's very difficult for her, but I give her a chance to do it. Often, it's not about making a task easier but being patient. We all need goals, after all. Something to work towards. And I know that if – no, *when* – Fran succeeds and pops the balloon, she'll be so happy. If I make the drill easier, she won't feel the same sense of achievement as she drenches me. And I want her to have the most powerful sense of achievement there is. The most powerful sense of joy and happiness through exercise.

I know I come up with some mad ideas sometimes – getting Josh to pretend to be a fish or annoying Kiera with a load of talcum powder. But there is always a point to it. Training people like Fran isn't about doing crazy drills that look great on Instagram or TikTok. That's not it. It's about making exercise possible, but also making them laugh and giving them normal experiences that will be useful in their everyday lives. It's about giving them fun, family experiences.

So, sometimes I'll get clients to paint my face, or I'll put shaving foam on and get them to try to shave me. If I put myself in stupid situations, where I look silly, I don't care. I'll do it happily, if it helps to put a smile on someone's face.

I remember putting boxing gloves on Fran and telling her that we had to train because she was going to fight Anthony Joshua. I had Fran hitting me hard with her right hand eight times. Then I asked her to give me a big left hook. That was tough for her, but she did it, because she's a fighter and a superstar. 'Anthony Joshua, we're coming for you!' I said on Instagram.

It helps on two levels. If Fran is bursting a balloon over my head, it's improving her mobility and co-ordination and shoulder stability. But it's more important that it's making her laugh.

YOU ARE A LEADER

And I don't mean fake laughs, just trying to disguise sadness. People doing that aren't really happy. They're pretending. But when I see one of my clients laughing from their stomach, uproariously, with their head tilted back, proper belly laughing . . . it's very, very special.

When I train people, I always make sure I have their attention from the start. I put myself out there. *I put on a performance.* There's no point in droning on to them, 'Right, we're doing a core stability exercise . . .' Instead, I put on a show. I tell a story. I entertain them. And they learn and they grow.

I'm an energy person. When I talk to you, from the second I open my mouth, I want to capture your attention. I know that I need action and interaction to learn and understand, and I think other people do, too.

I remember, when I was studying exercise and health sciences at Salford University, I thought it would be great to pick up a qualification in this area that I was so passionate about – but I absolutely *hated* it. This was mainly down to the style of teaching. It was just totally wrong for me. I hate having to sit down for a long time because my energy drops. I'm sure the lecturers were academically bright and had loads of qualifications, but they had no spark. They would stand and talk at us students for three hours in the same-monotonous-tone-of-voice-that-never-changed. There was no excitement, no variety, no nothing. Man, I found it boring!

YOU ARE NOT YOUR LIMITS

In one lecture, I actually fell asleep. I wasn't snoring (well, I hope not, anyway!) but the lecturer saw me and called out my name to wake me up.

'McLean!' he said. 'What did I just say?'

'I don't know,' I confessed.

'Come down to the front,' he ordered. I had to pick up my pens and papers and walk down and sit in the front row like a naughty kid. Bro, being right in front of the guy as he droned on was even worse! I only lasted a few minutes before I got up and began to walk back again.

'Where are you going?' the lecturer asked. I stopped and turned around. All the other students were looking at me.

'Entertain me!' I said. 'In order for me to learn anything, you need my attention. I've been sat here for two hours now and I can't remember one thing you've said. The only thing I remember is the boring tone of your voice. If you want me to learn, and not fall asleep, do more!'

Well, the lecturer looked gobsmacked by this. He kicked me out of the room and I had to go and see him the next day. Maybe he expected me to apologise for what I'd said to him. But I didn't. I doubled down.

'Your job as a teacher is to educate us but there has to be a degree of performance,' I told him. 'You have to perform.'

The guy looked at me as if I had two heads. '*Perform?*' he repeated. 'What do you think I am, a singer? A dancer?'

'No, but it's the same principle,' I said. 'You have to perform to captivate people and get their attention. Once

YOU ARE A LEADER

you've got my undivided attention, I will listen to you forever. But you're not doing that.'

Let's just say that the lecturer and I were not on the same page. He shook his head. That was the end of our meeting. I was sure he'd write to my mum and dad, and I knew they'd be livid. The next few weeks, I was on tenterhooks every morning when the post came: 'Nothing from my uni, is there, Mum?' Thankfully, the guy never wrote.

I've taken lessons from that bad experience and I always try to make sure that I grab people's attention when I am trying to teach them something, to put on a show to engage them. If you want to inspire people, you have to be creative and bring energy. You can't just stand there and drone on.

One of the most incredible things about Fran is her drive to inform and inspire people around the world about cerebral palsy. On her Instagram, she calls herself 'a badass warrior with cerebral palsy' and I love that. *You say it loud, girl!* You say it with volume and bass! You keep screaming it to the world because that's what you are.

Fran *is* a warrior with cerebral palsy. She's a leader. She's not afraid to put herself out there. She's not afraid to discuss every topic, every statement, every bullet point that she wants to raise. She's not afraid to let people know that she's in the room – and she's ready to talk and be heard.

FRANCESCA:

I laugh so much with Javeno because he gets me doing exercise, but it doesn't feel like real exercise. He makes it feel like it's a game. He makes it fun. For me, exercise always used to seem difficult and intimidating, but Javeno flips all that completely on its head. There's always music on and there's always a lot of laughing.

Then when the session's over, and I go home, during the week Javeno and his staff will be texting and messaging me, asking, 'Are you OK? Is there anything that we can help you with?' Having a friendship group like that . . . well, it's like winning the lottery.

I feel as if the other guys who train at J7 are my best friends. Family. We talk on our WhatsApp group. Before we went to Parklife, I was chatting on there with Aimee and Kiera, making plans: 'Right, what are you going to wear?'

I had a really tough time, personally, at the start of 2024. In January, I lost a really special friend, Megan. We'd met at a place called the Calvert Trust, in the Lake District, which provides holidays and activities for disabled people. Abseiling, canoeing, rock climbing: you name it, you can do it there.

Megan had severe cerebral palsy, like me, but she also had epilepsy which, unfortunately, meant that

YOU ARE A LEADER

she had a lot of seizures. She was nearly the same age as me: 27, just two years younger. We became very close but, sadly, she died. Her body just gave up on her.

It turned my world upside down. She was the first person with almost exactly the same condition as me that I'd lost. It was incredibly upsetting, and it meant so much, and helped so much, that my friends from J7 were there for me, talking to me on WhatsApp and over the phone.

Losing Megan also made me realise that you have to grab life by the balls because you never know what's going to happen. When she passed, I became really close friends with her family, and then I thought, you know what? I'm sick of the grief! I decided to turn a really negative thing into a positive.

In May 2024, my support worker and I did a half-marathon in Rawtenstall, near Burnley, where I live. It was such a great experience. The crowd were amazing and really cheered us on. We did it in three hours! Towards the end, the battery in my wheelchair died, so my poor support worker had to push me manually over the line!

Losing Megan has made me determined to keep working and make a difference. I feel so lucky that Javeno, and social media, give me that opportunity. Yet sometimes, when I look at Instagram and TikTok, it can feel quite surreal. Sometimes, I wonder if it's really happening.

I come from a small town in Lancashire where everybody knows one another, and yet I have people following me from Italy, and Spain, and Texas, and Nigeria. I don't get it. It sometimes makes me wonder, why are those people so interested in me? And yet I'm so glad that they are.

I've been on television five times. I get invited to go on podcasts. It can be daunting, but it allows me to deliver my message to young people and their parents that, yes, it's scary to get a diagnosis of cerebral palsy, or any other disability. But no matter how severe it is, there is always hope, with the right people and the right support.

I feel like I've been given a golden ticket, like in Charlie and the Chocolate Factory.

And long may it continue.

9.
LIFTING EACH OTHER UP

JOANNE:

In June 2023, when Tallulah was 11, she got diagnosed with acute lymphoblastic leukaemia, or ALL. She did five weeks of treatment in hospital and then she came home. But after three days, they called us back and said she had the Philadelphia gene, which is a very rare form of leukaemia.

If Lu had had straightforward ALL, she would have needed treatment for three years. But because she had this Philadelphia gene, the chemotherapy wasn't working. She had to start all this new treatment – immunotherapy and radiotherapy – and then she had to have a bone marrow transplant that October.

Tallulah was allowed home once she'd recovered, but she got graft-versus-host disease, where your body fights the transplant. She got very ill with that. She was back in the hospital until Christmas. They let her come home for Christmas Day.

She made it to New Year's Eve, but then she got sick with a cold because her immune system was so low. She got something called Guillain-Barré syndrome where, instead of her body fighting the cold, it fought itself. And that paralysed Lu from the waist down.

By the start of 2024, she could move her arms but the paralysis was moving up her body to her throat. She had to be given oxygen. She couldn't walk at all for six weeks. She started having seizures in hospital. Then she got meningitis in her spine. They gave her treatment for that and she had to learn how to walk again.

When Tallulah first got diagnosed, I had a friend, Jenny, who trained with Javeno at J7. She told him all about her, and he did a charity fundraiser for her.

Normally, if you're going to the gym, you think, oh no, I've got to go to the gym. When Tallulah had to go to physio in the hospital, she'd be like, oh no, not physio! But she gets excited to go and see Javeno because she knows she's going to have a good time. Because he's funny and he makes her laugh.

There's always laughing in his classes. Whether

LIFTING EACH OTHER UP

the cameras are on or off, he's such a positive, inspirational person. He doesn't only help Lu with her fitness. He helps with her confidence. When he tells her there's no such word as 'can't' and that she can do something, she believes him. And then she does it.

TALLULAH:

I was so sad in hospital. I was kept in one room and wasn't allowed out of it. I had to sit in the room for three months. I was poorly, so I was sleeping a lot, and I couldn't see my little brother and sister, Benny and Miley. Then, when I was paralysed, I had to be in my wheelchair all the time. I still can't walk long distances.

I liked Javeno when I first met him because he was funny. I liked how confident he was. I'd seen other physios and they'd always tell me, 'No, I wouldn't try to do that yet.' But Javeno was, like, 'Yeah, of course you can do it, girl! Come on, let's do it!' It's never 'no' with Javeno. I don't think he knows the word.

The first time I went to train, I was a bit nervous, but Javeno quickly took that feeling away. He made everything fun. He made me believe I could do things – even if, when he first asked me to do them, they seemed impossible.

He gave me a medicine ball and told me to throw

it over my shoulder. It was heavy and the first time I tried to do it, I couldn't. Nor the second time. But Javeno was encouraging me, until I thought, yeah, OK, I can do this! And then I managed it.

Another time, he got me to do squats over foam bricks. Every time I did it, he'd throw the bricks at my mum! It really made me laugh. Then he let me throw one at her, too. He makes my mum do exercise, as well as me. He tells her she has to do it, so that I can see her taking care of herself.

After I'd been going for a few weeks, Javeno got me running on a treadmill. Quite fast! And I thought, I couldn't even WALK at the start of this year!

Javeno is just like my big brother. He tells me off if I go to the gym in makeup. We have lots of fake arguments and banter and it makes us both laugh. I can do it because I'm so comfortable around him. It's like he's a member of my family.

Jenny was a regular client of mine and she told me all about her friend's lovely young daughter, Tallulah, who had this very rare form of leukaemia. She sounded like she had such a beautiful soul.

Jenny told me that Tallulah was in hospital on a ward with a few girls younger than her. They loved her Squishmallow toy and Tallulah told her mum she wished she could buy one for each of the little cancer survivors.

LIFTING EACH OTHER UP

I thought that was so sweet and noble. So we organised a fundraiser so she could buy every child in the ward a Squishmallow.

We held it in J7. It was an honour to do it. I did 1,000 bicep curl reps, along with a couple of other staff and some guys who come in to train. Tallulah came down to the event. She had a tube running from her nose to her mouth and was wearing a headscarf because the chemo had taken her hair. But she looked like an angel. I was so glad she was in the building.

I have to admit that after I met Tallulah and Joanne that time, I cried. I've never told them this. But I looked in Tallulah's eyes, had a chat with her and, later on, I had a good blub. I was crying at the unfairness of life. How cruel the world can be. How could this kind, beautiful little girl, with her whole life ahead of her, be dealt such a shitty hand? Why should she have to lose her hair, and undergo horrible medical treatment, and have to learn to walk again, when she should be laughing and playing with her friends?

I was really upset but I snapped out of it when I realised that Tallulah has a strength that is indescribable. She doesn't feel sorry for herself. So, I have no business feeling sorry for her either. Once I realised that, I started concentrating more on how I could help her achieve her goals.

After the fundraiser, I kept in touch with Tallulah's

mum. She asked me if I could train Tallulah in J7, once she was walking again and had been told she was safe to do exercise. I said, 'Hell, yeah! No doubt! A hundred million per cent!' Then I just waited for the text to tell me she was OK to start.

I remember Tallulah's first session. She was so nervous and scared – she was really young, remember, and had been through so much. I just wanted to make her feel comfortable as soon as she set foot in the centre. The atmosphere in J7 had to be right for her. Just like I do with everyone, I let Tallulah know that – while she might be young and had been unwell for a long period – she had as much right to be there as anybody else. Tallulah belongs at J7 just as much as all the other community members who come in.

Despite her nerves, Tallulah and I formed a bond quickly. I'm not going to lie – it's not always like that. Not all clients immediately become my best friends. Everyone is different, and with some people it takes a while to build a solid relationship. And then there are people with whom the rapport is just *instant*. Like Tallulah. As I said, she's a very special person.

*

I get that I am in a very privileged position because I get to see my superstars day in, day out, and witness their strength and sense of humour and all the brilliant stuff

LIFTING EACH OTHER UP

they achieve. But still, it blows my mind sometimes that, out there in society, there are people who can't seem to see what I see in them.

I'm protective towards the guys I train. I hope that's not patronising – I don't think it is. If you care about someone, you're always going to want to stand up for them, to back them. If I ever feel like they're getting disrespected, I'll fight their corner for them, even if they don't want to be fought for, or they don't even know that I'm doing it. And there was a good example of that recently.

Josh gets brought to the gym with his carer in taxis that have big spaces at the back for disabled people. A few weeks ago, he came in for his session. I had to leave afterwards to go to a meeting and when I came back, three hours later, Joshy was still sitting there in the gym. *Huh? What's going on?*

His carer told me the taxi had pulled up and the driver had taken one look at Josh out of the window, said something like, 'Nah, I don't want that big dirty wheelchair in here!' and driven off. The carer called the cab firm office to complain, and they put the phone down on her. Josh was stuck at J7 for hours and hours.

A couple of weeks later, one of my female disabled clients had the same thing happen at Manchester Piccadilly station. An adapted cab had pulled into the rank but the driver told her, 'No, not today, love. Not in that thing.' *What?* I went on my socials and had a bit of a rant. But that didn't feel like enough. So, I went down to the taxi firm's head office.

I was *fuming*. I was not a nice person in that office. I told them, 'It's disgusting! I'm not having it! How dare you treat individuals like that!' They were a bit shocked to have a raging madman suddenly arrive in their reception. They apologised and promised it wouldn't happen again.

I see it as part of my job. I will fight my guys' corner. If I see injustice against them, I'll do whatever it takes for people to understand the error of their ways. I try to stand up for the people society can forget or belittle or patronise or discriminate against.

I've always felt strongly about this, from when I was a kid. I loved my bit of Manchester growing up (and still do!), but I can't deny that it could be pretty rough. There was a nasty element to it. I mostly really enjoyed high school but there was also something I hated: the racism I saw there. I was at school in the late nineties and there was a lot of it about. There weren't many Black kids in my school. I never got grief personally because I've always been very confident and I had a lot of mates, so nobody was going to come up and say something bad to my face. They knew I wouldn't tolerate it. But some kids had a horrible time.

I had a couple of Asian friends who were regularly bullied and racially abused. Some kids were always in their faces, calling them names and slapping them about. They'd get dragged into bushes. Once, one of them got tied

LIFTING EACH OTHER UP

to a bus stop. I used to try my best to protect them: 'Oi! You mess with them, you mess with me!' But I couldn't always be there. We were exposed early on to the world's harsh way of marginalising people because they were different.

One Friday, when I was about 13, I was away from school for the day to play cricket for the North of England in Scarborough and I couldn't stop thinking about my two Asian mates. I knew when school finished at three o'clock and I wasn't there, they were going to face abuse. I felt sick.

And I was right: when I saw my friends, they told me they'd been chased from the bus stop through a park and hit and kicked by 15 or 20 kids. It had been nasty. Brutal.

I just didn't understand . . . how can people do that? I still don't understand and I never will. I know, on a basic level, that people can be scared of anyone who looks different from them. But it made me feel both angry and powerless. I felt guilty that I hadn't been there to protect my mates. I just felt, *I wouldn't have let that happen.*

There was another young Black kid in my school who got severely bullied. He was a really nice, well-mannered lad but small in stature and quite vulnerable, and kids knew they could abuse him. And they did. I'll never forget, one day, asking him, 'Hey, how you doing?' And he told me he'd been called the N-word 45 times that day. He'd been counting.

The racism got so bad that his mum had to take him

out of the school. And the horrible thing is, that kind of experience can change a person's life in a very destructive way. That kid never got over the way he was treated at school. He went on to a life of drugs and crime, got involved with gangs and became very violent. This is why safe spaces are so important. For people who have experienced any kind of trauma, there needs to be an outlet or a community they can be part of.

I still see that guy regularly around Blackley and talk to him. The hatred he has for some people, and what they did to him at school, is extreme. And I can understand why. He'll never forgive them. The kids who used to abuse him have probably forgotten all about it, or think it was a bit of fun. They don't realise how badly they damaged his life.

My time in high school taught me that the smallest thing, the slightest comment, can change someone's life, in a great way, or a terrible way. And I've always known that I never want to be a person who makes a negative, disgusting comment that destroys someone. I want to do the exact opposite. We need to lift each other up. Especially those who have not been treated kindly in life.

Now and then, one of my superstars has told me they feel like a burden. I've always bollocked them. 'You're not a burden!' I'll say. 'Never! When you come to J7, I'll move every bit of equipment that's in your way. Any of us able-bodied guys will do the same! You're *not* a burden!'

But if you regularly had experiences like Josh and my

LIFTING EACH OTHER UP

other client did with the taxis, or our little gang did at Parklife, before they sorted it out, then you might well feel like a burden sometimes. It's so unfair.

I got a small insight into how that can feel in summer 2024 when I got another of my occasional sports injuries. I smashed my leg up (again!) in a charity football match in Manchester. Twelve years after I ruptured the Achilles tendon in my left leg playing squash with Ty and had to hobble around in a space boot, just to even things up, I snapped the one in my right.

This time, though, the injury meant that I had to be in a wheelchair for about three weeks before I could even progress to wearing a surgical boot. The docs told me to rest up at home and not go anywhere. But I hate letting anybody down. I just can't do it. So, I got taxis and carried on going into the gym to train my superstars. I believe that you can always create something good from any situation in life. Whatever experiences I have, good or bad, I try to find some positivity in them. If anything, being in a wheelchair fuelled my creativity and I devised some sessions that I could take while I was in the chair.

I got Josh and Paul in and did a couple of wheelchair races against them. I lost – badly! Very badly. I may pride myself on being a powerlifter and a strong guy, but it takes a different kind of strength to power a wheelchair. Even when I tried to work out ways to cheat, I couldn't get anywhere near them.

YOU ARE NOT YOUR LIMITS

It was an eye-opening experience. I was privileged in that I knew it was only temporary, so there's no way I can really compare it, but it definitely gave me a new understanding of what it's like for some of my clients. I have been training disabled people for more than 20 years and I've always had sympathy and empathy for them. But this experience increased it a thousand-fold. For the first time, I got a glimpse of life from their perspective and realised how incredibly hard it is.

I saw the disrespect and the dirty looks that people in wheelchairs get. I saw how little thought society gives to disabled people when it comes to accessibility – with simple things, like installing ramps or dropped kerbs. I saw the way they get treated as lesser beings. I saw the world the way my guys see it, and what they have to battle against just to get through the day.

And yes, in that wheelchair, for the first time in my life, I felt like a burden. Now I could see why even my toughest superstars would sometimes say that to me. And why me trying to reassure them wasn't enough. I believe that we have created a magical, inclusive space at J7. But out there, in the world, I often felt like a nuisance. An irritation. I felt like I was constantly in people's way and they didn't want me around. Like I was making life difficult for everyone. And it gave me an infinite amount of respect for my guys who are made to feel like that every single day.

LIFTING EACH OTHER UP

Just after I ruptured my Achilles, Laura and I went away for the weekend for our wedding anniversary. We went to a beautiful British city for a spa break and some sightseeing. When I was there, I had a really tough time in my wheelchair. It was such a struggle.

The city has a castle so we went to have a gawp at it. But it was impossible for me to get around it. Some areas had no disabled access at all. Other bits had signs next to paths saying 'disabled access' – but the path just led to steps! I mean, had nobody who worked there ever bothered to walk down the path and see the problem?

I was fuming, so I tackled a member of staff about it. He could not have cared less. He was blasé. It made me wonder: has he never dealt with disabled people before? Is he oblivious to their needs? Does he just not give a shit because it doesn't affect his own life? Because, sadly, too many people are like that.

I asked him why they couldn't put hydraulic platforms in the castle for wheelchair users. He said it's a historical building, so they can't touch it. It wasn't until he'd gone that I thought, *oh yeah? Well, you put electricity and a gift shop in, didn't you? They weren't there in medieval times!*

Unfortunately, a lot of disadvantaged people feel they can't speak up. I've got a big gob, so I pulled that dude and let him have it. But a lot of disabled people can't be arsed to fight their shit treatment because it's exhausting to have to do that *every day*. They've had it so many times they're used to it. Which is an awful situation but they just accept it as their lot.

Later, Laura and I went to a coffee shop in the city. I immediately wanted to leave. The aisles were too narrow and I couldn't get down them. I was banging into things and knocking stuff over. I saw people rolling their eyes and tutting. I felt like I was in everyone else's way. I'd never felt like that before. It was horrible.

We went into a clothes shop and I parked up in my wheelchair, near the shirts, to wait for Laura. People were hovering and waiting for me to go before they browsed the shirts. They glared at me as if I had some disease. They looked uncomfortable. I had to say to them, 'It's OK! You can come near me, you know!'

We'd be in a lift, just the two of us. It would stop at a floor and the people waiting would look in the door, shake their heads and say, 'Don't worry, we'll wait for the next one.' And I'd look all around me and say, 'There's loads of space in here. You can come in! I don't bite!' And they *still* wouldn't come in.

There were so many indignities. A few were intentional but most were just thoughtless. I got obsessed with spotting them. Laura and I went to a cool jazz bar. It had seven steps leading up to the entrance and no ramp. I was able to get out of my wheelchair, leave it outside and hobble up on my crutches. But most people in chairs can't do that.

LIFTING EACH OTHER UP

Once we were inside, we had some nice food and then I had to go to the toilet. I looked around and saw a sign: 'disabled toilet'. *Huh?* I thought. *What are you talking about? If you're in a wheelchair, you can't even get in this bloody bar!* They were just ticking a box to get their council licence. But it was meaningless. An insult.

They also had a disabled toilet at the spa, but even there, it wasn't fit for purpose. I could wheel my chair in, but there wasn't enough space to shut the door. Just like Josh's experience at Parklife. I had to do my business with the door wide open. It was so humiliating. Again, had no one who worked there ever bothered to check their facilities?

Overall, it was really hard to enjoy our break. Every single time I got out of my car and had to use my wheelchair, it upset me. Because all I could think was: *this is what my guys go through, every day of their lives.* I was relieved to get out of my wheelchair after about three weeks. The docs gave me a big surgical boot and told me to wear it for three to four months.

*

I don't do many group sessions with my superstars. I train them one-to-one because their needs are so varied. People with different levels of cerebral palsy, say, or spina bifida, have different capabilities, even though they have the same condition. Aimee is different to Josh, who is different to Fran. I give them the respect they deserve by devising bespoke individual lessons. But they're all such good mates that I'll occasionally get a few of them in for a joint class. And one lunchtime, while I still had my big boot on, I did a group session with Josh, Aimee and Paul. Being in the wheelchair was still on my mind, so I told them all about the shit I'd had.

And you know what was depressing? They weren't surprised. None of them. They just listened to me and nodded, because they've all had the same treatment, or worse, a thousand times before. And then they started telling their own horror stories. And they had *a lot*.

Aimee told us that she's been to loads of places with 'disabled access' signs but no actual disabled access. 'So I can't get in,' she said. 'I'll find someone who works there. I'll ask, "What are you going to do about this?" And they just shrug and say, "There's nothing I can do."'

'Which is another way of saying, "We can't be bothered,"' said Josh.

'That's right,' Aimee agreed. 'Plenty of times, my mum's had to actually lift me out of my chair and carry me up steps. And you feel such a burden.' (That word again.)

'I went to a karaoke bar in Leeds,' said Paul. 'I was with a group of mates on a night out. The bouncer told me: "You can't come in. We haven't got facilities for your type." I ask you! *Your type?!* I said, "I'll just use the facilities you've got, then." But he still wouldn't let me in.'

LIFTING EACH OTHER UP

Another regular at the gym had overheard and joined in our conversation. He had a bad story. 'I went to Canada once,' he said. 'They only sent one old guy to help put me on the plane. Obviously, I'm a big lad, so it needs more than that. It meant the flight was delayed by about 40 minutes. I felt awful but it wasn't my fault.

'They eventually managed to get me on the plane and into my seat. I was sitting there, waiting for take-off, and a member of the cabin crew came walking down the aisle with an angry passenger. She stopped next to my seat, pointed at me, and told the guy, "*This* is why you're delayed."'

Wow! That's so rude and embarrassing. But these slights to the disabled community aren't normally deliberate or malicious. Often it's just thoughtlessness. Carelessness. Laziness. It's part of a complex unconscious bias that has built up over years of discrimination, passed down through generations. People not thinking properly about the facilities they need to provide. And yet I've seen first-hand how these things can be rectified.

*

In 2024, Tallulah came in and told me that she'd rung the bell in the hospital. This meant she had finished her treatment and was free of cancer. That was such a special moment. It made my heart and soul smile so much. I was so proud of her and so pleased that there is a new,

'It's part of a complex unconscious bias that has built up over years of discrimination, passed down through generations.'

LIFTING EACH OTHER UP

fantastic chapter of her life coming up now. And that is exactly what she deserves.

One of my main goals with Tallulah, ever since that first time she anxiously walked in, was to show her how much she is capable of doing. To prove to her just how much is possible and how much she can achieve. Well, she's achieved so much, and now she can go on and achieve even more. The sky's the limit.

TALLULAH:

When Javeno had his big boot on after he broke his leg, he made me run all the way around the outside of the gym. All the way around the car park. When I came back in, I told him that he had to do it next. We made a bet that we'd do a race when he was totally better, because I think I'm faster than him now.

I love going to J7 because of Javeno but also because I've got friends there. Aimee is really nice. I met her when we went to Parklife. And Fran is lovely. In the hospital, I met a girl called Sophia, who was the only person there with the exact same rare kind of leukaemia as well. She goes to J7 too.

I really like reading the lovely messages that people from all over the world leave me. They say, 'Kick it!' or 'Go, Tallulah!' or they tell me that they really enjoy seeing me on Javeno's page. That encourages me and helps me to do better.

YOU ARE NOT YOUR LIMITS

In 2024, I rang the bell in the hospital to say that I was clear of cancer. It was brilliant. We had a big party at home. I'm still learning to do certain things. I'm learning how to eat again. I still have some procedures that make me feel sick. I'm still having naps in the day. But I'm getting there.

Javeno and J7 have helped me so much. They gave me my strength back. They gave me my confidence back. And I know that I'm stubborn anyway, but Javeno has made me even more stubborn . . .

JOANNE:

Javeno can see Tallulah's potential, just like a parent can. After Lu had had five or six sessions with him, it was like they'd known each other forever. It's great that they have that relationship because once or twice I've had to ask him to give her a little motivational talk.

Tallulah had to have a catheter in when she was in hospital with Guillain-Barré syndrome, and it really affected her bladder. When she came out, if she tried to walk long distances, she felt as if she needed the toilet all the time. So she got a little bit used to, and comfy with, using her wheelchair rather than working at her walking.

In 2024, she had a trip to America coming up where there was going to be a lot of walking. So I

LIFTING EACH OTHER UP

messaged Javeno to say, 'Can you please give Lu a bit of a pep talk, because I'm worried she's not walking enough.' And next time he saw her, he said, 'You've been lazy, you! You need to start doing more! You don't need the wheelchair. You can walk!'

10.
ABSORBING THE PAIN AND BRINGING THE SUNSHINE

You might think, given all the people who come to the gym, and how well-known it's getting, and the social media love we get, that things couldn't be better for J7. And that's true, in a way. I don't know if I have said it enough yet – I am so proud of what everyone who comes to J7, both staff and clients, have achieved. It truly is the magical place I imagined when I was sitting at my mum's kitchen table, biro in hand, all that time ago. And then some. But what I do isn't all non-stop happiness and euphoria. It can't be. Let me tell you, I've cried a lot doing this job, over the people who come here.

How could I not? There has been so much heartbreak. How many youngsters have I known who've had cancers, and degenerative diseases, and been given six months to live? How many people did I lose to Covid? How many of my elderly clients have passed away in recent years?

I see the struggles people are *really* going through, which you don't see on social media. I see disabled youngsters hurting from being disrespected and belittled by society. I see the pain and difficulties of disadvantaged people who don't have it easy in life and, due to the conditions they were born with, never have had, and never will.

How do I help them and lift them? I train them with a heart that is full of love and care. I keep my positivity turned up so high that it goes right through the roof, then keeps going. I try to give them my full focus and create sessions that will lift them out of any lethargy or depression and get them motivated again.

It isn't always easy, though. Two years ago, one of my clients was going through some terrible stuff in their personal life. They told me all about it, all the horrible details, and it really affected me. It really choked me up.

We had a good, private heart-to-heart in the gym and then we had an amazing session. I could see it had really lifted them. But after they'd left, I still felt so emotional. I went outside, sat in my car and burst into tears. Because when you love somebody, you hate to see them going through something like that. You can't bear it.

After I'd let it all out and sorted myself out, I came back in the gym and I called them up. I checked they were

ABSORBING THE PAIN AND BRINGING THE SUNSHINE

OK and then I told them, 'Just to let you know, whatever happens, I've got you. I've got your back. You know I'm always here.'

I feel as if my job is to absorb people's pain. Absorb the pain of my young, beautiful clients suffering disabilities and degenerative illnesses. I can't avoid being emotionally involved, but I *can* absorb the pain and channel it into something different, so they can laugh and smile again. That's how to get pure joy.

I love Aimee, I love Noah, I love DJ, I love Kiera, I love Marley, I love Shania, I love Sophia. I love them all. I love training them and I love seeing them get stronger and more confident. And my passion for what I do gets stronger all the time, because my love for them gets deeper and deeper.

But with love can come loss. That's how life works, sadly. It's inevitable, given that I work with so many elderly clients and people with terminal illnesses, that I'm going to see a lot of people I've grown to know, love and come to view as friends, pass away.

Well, it's natural, but that doesn't make it any easier to deal with.

I used to train a middle-aged cancer sufferer. He was a smashing guy, and we had a laugh and a good craic every session. I used to look forward to seeing him. Then, one week, he came in and said he'd come straight from having hospital tests and they'd told him he had seven months to live.

YOU ARE NOT YOUR LIMITS

The news hit me like a sledgehammer. I gave him a hug and told him I was popping out to get something and I'd be right back. I went outside, stood by the chemist shop next to J7 and totally lost my shit. I leaned against the shop wall and I cried and I cried.

I must have looked a real sight: a big, strapping bloke, standing outside a chemist, sobbing my heart out. A couple of people walked past, saw me and came over: 'Are you alright, luv? What's up? Can I help?'

I said, 'No, no, I'm OK, thanks!' And, after they'd gone, I gave myself a good slap.

Fucking hell, what's going on here? I thought. *What am I doing? It's not about me. This poor guy has just told me he's got seven months to live. What the fuck am I crying for, and making it all about me? What can I do to make this man's life better, right now, in the present? Think, Javeno! What can I do?*

I devised a good session for the guy right there and then, in my head, then went back in and did it with him. He enjoyed it and he was laughing. After he'd gone, I gave myself another talking to: *Sort it out! Why am I letting myself cry, when someone else is going through something a million times worse than my feelings?*

Sadly, he didn't even get to live out those next seven months. He passed away after just four. It was hard for everyone who knew him.

One client whose passing really upset me was the lovely

ABSORBING THE PAIN AND BRINGING THE SUNSHINE

Aunty Veronica, the Irish lady I used to play Irish jigs for while she trained. One week, she was coming to J7 for a group class and asked if she could have a word. We went into my little office, and she told me that she had cancer and she didn't have long to live.

Aunty Veronica shed a few tears. I did the same, but I was trying to hold it together. Then she wiped her eyes, said, 'On with the show, son!' and we went out and did the class. She was such a beautiful lady. I still have a photograph of her on the wall of J7, to make sure that her memory lives on.

I used to train a local lollipop man, Jim, with his wife Monica and their daughter, Paula. All three of them came to a circuit training class on Fridays for years. They were a great family. I grew close to all of them. Jim and Monica have sadly both passed away.

Whenever Jim came in and trained in the class, he always did it in the same corner of the gym. I used to call it 'Jim's Corner'. Because he was such a well-known character, the local newspaper ran a story about him when he died. I cut it out, got it framed, and now it hangs on the J7 wall in Jim's Corner. It's my tribute.

One of my ladies had me in bits one day when she came in with terrible news. She was only in her thirties. She had been training with me for about a year as part of her rehab while she recovered from breast cancer. She had been in remission and it seemed like things were looking good.

YOU ARE NOT YOUR LIMITS

That lady was so strong. Real strength isn't bicep curls or bench presses or squats. It's not in your muscles. It's in your heart. You don't count real strength in kilograms. Real strength is internal, when people are fighting their demons and their emotions and their fears. When they're fighting a disease that they can't even see.

The lady hadn't been in to train for about two months. I'd missed her. Then she turned up at J7 out of the blue one morning. She hadn't got a session booked and she wasn't due to train. I was on my computer in my poky office and she knocked on my door: 'Hello? Javeno?'

Man, I was so pleased to see her! I gave her a big hug and said, 'Where have you been? How are you getting on? Have you had any more test results from the hospital? When are you coming in to train again?' And she didn't answer. Didn't say a single word. She just looked at me, shook her head, and started crying.

And I knew.

I started crying as well. She hugged me again. I hugged her back. She didn't tell me that she had been given a terminal prognosis but she didn't need to. It was written all over her face. 'I still want you to come in,' I told her, between gulps. But she still didn't say anything. She just looked at me and smiled.

She smiled, and left, and I knew that she had come in one last time to say goodbye. It was the worst. It made me feel so angry. I thought: *Fucking hell, man! It's so unfair!*

ABSORBING THE PAIN AND BRINGING THE SUNSHINE

This is a kind, loving lady, with a family, with young children – how can she be chosen to die?

After she'd gone, I felt true pain. This was a friend that I was close to, that I'd laughed with, shared jokes with, and hugged a hundred times. The look on her face broke my heart. It was real pain. Because real pain isn't loud or in your face. Real pain is a silent killer that crushes you from the inside.

I cried so much that day. I don't know how I kept it together in my sessions with my clients. I had to practise what I preach and show real strength, the kind that you don't measure in kilograms. I had to take strength from how strong *she* was. But when I got home that night, I took myself off and I cried again. I cried till I was all cried out.

It goes with what I do. Sometimes, I have to look death in the face. Nobody wants to die. That lady certainly didn't want to die; I could see it in her eyes. But she was still strong. I was honoured, and grateful, that she'd come in to say goodbye to me. It was so fucking sad, and it made me think: *I'm always going to do what I do. I'm never going to stop.* Because people in that situation need help more than anybody in the world.

*

There's another lady in J7 at the moment who exemplifies exactly why I need to keep doing what I do. She's a stroke survivor who's been coming here for three or four months.

YOU ARE NOT YOUR LIMITS

She's been working so hard, she's cried so many tears and she's sometimes wanted to give up.

This woman has questioned her capability so many times. She's dissected her character and her personality in a manner that has been hard to watch. She's told me, 'I don't think I'm as mentally strong as I thought I was. I used to never give up, but maybe that's just not me anymore.' It's heartbreaking to hear.

What do I do when she says things like that? I ignore it. I absorb her pain. I know she's got it in her to keep fighting and I'm willing to play the long game with her. I don't give up on people. I've seen her shed so many tears and we've shared so many hugs. I'll never stop lifting her up: 'Come on! Keep your chin up, girl!'

That woman has given so much, both emotionally and physically, to win back two inches of movement in her stroke-affected arm. But she works, she gets there, and then she smiles in a pure, beautiful way, born of effort and dedication. And it makes the pain worthwhile. For both of us.

*

It's such a tragedy, but there are people all over the world who decide that they don't want to go on living. In 2024, a lady in Florida messaged me and told me about her multiple health problems. She was all alone, her family hadn't come to see her in six or seven weeks, and she said that she had decided to end her life.

ABSORBING THE PAIN AND BRINGING THE SUNSHINE

The lady said she had made her decision and she was comfortable and at peace with it. And why was she telling me, a stranger, thousands of miles away in England? She said she'd watched the J7 videos and if I were in Florida, she'd come to see me and I would be the only reason she'd want to be alive.

Man! What do you do when you get a message like that? How do you respond? I longed to do a Zoom with her, or FaceTime, but after she left the message for me, she deleted her account. I had no way of reaching out to her. Receiving that sad, sad message, I felt all kinds of emotions . . . and the main one was guilt.

I knew, deep down, that if I could reach that woman, I could help her. I could distract her, be present with her and make her laugh. I could bring some love, and some energy, into her life and, hopefully, at the end she would think, *you know what? This being alive isn't so bad! Let's give it another go!*

I wish I could have done a session with her and brought her some joy.

I wish I could have helped her.

I hope that lady is OK.

*

When I was setting up the J7 health centre back in 2017, aside from painting the centre orange, I also decided to put statues of the Buddha around the place. There's a big one in reception and others scattered all around the gym. I'm not a Buddhist, as such, but when I was in India, I fell in love with the teachings of *dharma*. There is a doctrine around dukkha, which means that life induces suffering. And the antidote to suffering is to help others and be unselfish.

It is also important to be grateful for what you have. When I think back to my earliest memories in Jamaica, before we moved to the UK, I don't remember poverty. I remember sunny days, being by the ocean and playing with my friends. I remember happiness, not hardship. But I know we didn't have much and my parents worked very hard for us. Jamaica is a beautiful country, as anybody who has been there on a sunshine holiday can tell you. It looks like paradise. But that doesn't mean that everyone who comes from there is leading a heavenly life – it's a poor country with more than its share of unfairness and social problems.

As a kid, I loved *The A Team* and I once saw Mr T being interviewed. He looked smart but he had raggedy shoes on. A cocky Hollywood reporter was taking the mick out of him about about his shoes but Mr T put him in his place: 'I wear these shoes to remind myself where I came from, and to humble myself,' he said. I'll never forget that. And that is how I see Jamaica and my roots.

I've been back to Jamaica as a grown man and it's a wonderful place, full of some of the kindest souls

ABSORBING THE PAIN AND BRINGING THE SUNSHINE

you could ever meet. The tourist areas, like Montego Bay, are gorgeous. But coming from there has taught me to be grateful for everything. Because a bad day in England would be perfection compared to life in some other places.

I think sometimes we've just got to ask ourselves – did you have breakfast this morning? Do you have running water? Have you got stairs in your house? Have you got a bed? Of course we do. But asking ourselves questions like this reminds us to be thankful and reframe our mindset when we are moaning about having a bad night's sleep or slow traffic, and letting what basically amounts to a minor inconvenience cast a shadow over our whole day. It's a reminder that there are many people who haven't been as lucky in life.

I apply the same principle of gratitude to being able-bodied. Able-bodied people should always be grateful that they can get up and walk, or sit down and cross their legs, or turn their neck, or scratch their nose. I know it's easy to take these things for granted when we do them multiple times a day, but so many guys that I train don't have those blessings. Every morning when I wake up, gratitude is the first and most powerful feeling for me.

Like a lot of people, the Covid lockdown reinforced this for me. It reminded me how vital health is, physical *and* mental. It taught me how vulnerable we all are, as human beings. It taught me to slow down and be grateful for the

YOU ARE NOT YOUR LIMITS

wonderful things we have: homes, beds, food, clothes. Loved ones. Never to take that stuff for granted.

Whenever I look at the Buddhas in the gym, it reminds me to 1) be myself, 2) treat others with respect and good manners, and put them first and 3) be grateful.

11.
WHAT'S NEXT?

The elite human beings who let me train them in J7 would be superstars even if nobody outside the gym walls ever saw the miracles they perform week after week. But, in fact, they are actual global superstars because social media transports them into people's homes all over the world.

Our social media figures nowadays are colossal. I've been told that, at the time of writing, we have 1.4 million followers on TikTok. The most popular video – Kiera walking from her car into J7 – has had 23 million views. In total, the videos we have shot during sessions, and then stuck online, have been viewed more than 100 million times. *100 million!*

It's so crazy that it can be hard to get my head around it sometimes. I'll admit there have been times when I've thought, *bloody hell, how has THAT happened?* As I said earlier, we never expected it when we first started whacking videos up online. We hoped to inspire a few people who might be going through similar struggles, but we could never have anticipated the outpouring of love from our now established community. Like all the best things in life, it's happened naturally.

When I give it some thought, I realise that each one-minute clip is a little story, a little movie, full of action scenes and heroism. And they always have a happy ending. With so much negativity online, our social media page can offer the same feeling as the health centre itself: it's a place where you can come and be uplifted and inspired.

The J7 superstars love going online and hearing from thousands of people saying wonderful things about them. Aimee and Kiera and Fran and Tallulah come into J7 *glowing* as they tell me about the encouraging messages that someone in Texas, or India, or Peru has sent them. It makes them so happy.

And it's not just the kids! My older clients have got their fans too. The other week, a lady who is a regular at my OAP class came in with her daughter. The daughter had looked at TikTok and seen people in Canada and Australia raving about how amazing her mother was. She was gobsmacked. 'Oh my God!' she told me. 'My mum's famous!'

This is all brilliant, of course, but I have to admit that when our social media first started taking off, I wasn't sure what to do. My focus has always been on training

WHAT'S NEXT?

people. Nothing else. But suddenly I was getting so many messages, texts and emails requesting that I do interviews, or podcasts, or this, that and the other, that I couldn't cope.

I'd done some interview stuff before. J7 had been in the *Manchester Evening News* a few times and we'd had local TV news camera crews at the gym. But now there was a completely different level of interest, and it wasn't just local or just national – it was international. I wanted to help as many people as possible, but I am just one person! I can't be everywhere at once. And how would I know what I should be saying yes to? I have to prioritise J7 and my guys above all else. But if I could spread the message of community and exercise for all even further, then at least some of these opportunities had to be worth it. But which ones?

I had to accept that I needed some help. And I knew it was time to bring somebody else on to the team.

I first started training a really friendly and determined young woman named Hayley nearly 20 years ago. Hayley used to come to my council classes, then she moved with me to J7 to be a PT client. She has been an actress, she's done event management and now she runs a media company with her partner Nik, who makes music and is well-known around Manchester.

I found that every time Hayley came down to J7, I was asking her advice: 'Some guy has asked me to do something and I'm not sure about it – what should I do?' 'I've been asked to go on a weird podcast – what do you think?' I always valued Hayley's opinion because she knew her stuff and she was a mate, with my best interests at heart.

Eventually, when I realised I needed a manager, there was only one person I wanted to ask. Hayley is family: she knows me inside out, she knows the values at J7, she knows my family. 'You're the only person I trust with this stuff,' I told her. 'Please, will you manage me?'

When Hayley said, '100 per cent! I'd love to!' I was delighted. And relieved. Because when you get a little bit well-known, even if – or maybe *especially* if – you never wanted to, it brings complications. The world of fame and celebrity, even at the low level I'm at, brings all sort of attention, both positive and negative. When you're not used to it, it can be confusing to deal with.

It's a weird thing. Hayley keeps me up to date with what's happening, and my J7 guys are always reading me comments off Instagram and TikTok, but I hardly ever look at my socials myself. *Never*, really. People leave lovely comments but I don't read them because I don't want my mind, and my focus, to be distracted.

Hayley and everybody else tell me that the comments on J7's Instagram and TikTok are 99.99999 per cent positive but, even so, we get a few haters. There are always going to be keyboard warriors, spewing out nasty thoughts, because . . . well, God knows why. I don't know how anybody could possibly hate on what we do at J7. But

WHAT'S NEXT?

some people do. These trolls don't know how much I love my clients. They don't know anything. They say stupid stuff like, 'Javeno's only doing all that for the cameras. I bet he's not like that in real life. He's just doing it for the likes.'

It's crazy. *How can people be so wrong?* But there's nothing I can do about negativity like that. So, I don't engage with it. I just ignore it. I don't even read it anymore. All I care about is training my guys. Nothing else matters. And for me to keep doing that, and to keep giving them the love and attention they deserve, and to keep planning sessions to the level that I am, I can't be derailed. Helping my guys is what I do. Everything else is just background noise.

I know some people get into certain lines of work because they want to get famous. But that's never been my intention. I take any 'celebrity' crap chucked at me with a pinch of salt. It doesn't mean anything to me. It's not going to change my life. You get to a point where you realise what actually makes you happy and what genuine kindness looks like.

My focus will always be on my mission: training people, helping people. That's the path I will always focus on. If the 'celebrity' stuff ended today . . . so what? I'd still be here, training Aimee, and Kiera, and Josh, and Noah. J7 would still be here. And I'm not about to give them up to go on *Strictly Come Dancing* or *Celebrity Bake Off*, lol!

YOU ARE NOT YOUR LIMITS

I'll do stuff like going on TV, writing this book and doing my socials, because I know how many Joshes and Kieras and Tallulahs it might reach around the world. If I can help to inspire them, or be a voice for them, I'll keep on doing media stuff. Just don't expect to see me eating bugs in the jungle with Ant and Dec, OK?

*

In 2023, I did the biggest media appearance I'd ever done. I flew to New York to be a guest on *Sherri*, a daytime talk show hosted by a woman named Sherri Shepherd. Sherri had seen my social media vids, I was on her show once via Zoom, and then she invited me to New York to talk about J7 and empowering disabled people.

Sherri is one of the most popular talk shows on American TV and is watched by a million people a day, but I wasn't nervous about going on because I would be talking about my work. I'm like anybody else: I can get nervous and uncomfortable about certain things. But I never do when it comes to my work.

As I was standing in the wings, waiting to walk out to a live TV audience, I thought, *you won't get heard if you don't speak.* I'm always going to speak out loudly for disabled people who get neglected and disrespected. Realistically, I'm always going to be the loudest voice in any room! So it makes sense to use that voice for the people I'm supporting.

WHAT'S NEXT?

*

Another amazing opportunity came around in 2024 – I got invited to Paris by Channel 4 to help them broadcast the Paralympics to the world. It was an honour and a privilege for me to attend such a special event and it was an absolutely fantastic experience.

I took my dad with me and we filmed what we got up to for Channel 4. We began with breakfast on the Eurostar, then did a bit of sightseeing: the Eiffel Tower, the Arc de Triomphe. Then we went to the Stade de France, watched the main athletics day, and did a load more filming. Being given that degree of freedom to big up the greatest show on earth was unbelievable. I felt so lucky.

I know a few Paralympians through social media. I'm friends with Lauren Steadman, the brilliant pentathlete. She got a bronze medal. I also know David Weir, the wheelchair athlete. He's supported my work for years and I'm a big fan of his, so it was amazing to be in the stadium to watch him compete.

Man, let me tell you this. Seeing all those incredible Paralympians with my own eyes, as I was doing for the first time, I was blown away. They were even more spectacular, motivational and inspirational than I could have imagined. Being right up close to them emphasised just how incredible human beings can be.

These athletes – some with very challenging issues

with mobility, balance and vision – were performing at an elite level on a sporting field. Their disabilities had not stopped them doing what they wanted to do or being what they wanted to be. And it was all shaped by care and love.

This kind of care and love doesn't just help people. It *moulds* them. All those Paralympians had received care and love, from the right people at the right time, along their journey. That had been the fuel that had led them through to these big moments on the global stage.

I sat with Dad in the Stade de France and we watched the fabulous young Karisma Evi Tirani break the world record for the women's 100m. We saw amazing javelin throwers and long jumpers. I sat back, soaked everything in, and saw a million things that made me smile, inside and out.

Like I said earlier, real strength is on the inside. And you have to get it out. You have to shed a few layers to expose the real strength inside. Those Paralympians had shed so many layers. They embodied unbreakable strength, talent and resilience. And that in itself is something to applaud.

There was one moment when I just sat there in the Stade de France and thought, *this is how the world should be. A place where everyone is celebrated. A place where real strength starts from within. A place where we support each other on our journeys. A place where you see, first-hand, that anything is possible.*

WHAT'S NEXT?

The Paralympics' organisation was mind-blowing. I'm used to seeing disabled people putting up with shit every day. At the Stade de France, every facility – ramps, doors, toilet access, people on hand to help – was absolutely spot on. Here was *true* disabled access. This should be the model that everything else is based on. It was wonderful.

*

As the health centre continues to grow, we're faced with challenges. Literally hundreds and hundreds of people want to come down and train with us. Which would be wonderful – except that they can't. Because I'm only one man and we're only one little orange gym behind a parade of shops in Blackley, Manchester. Currently, we don't have the resources to meet the demand. The demand that absolutely proves that there is a large demographic of people who are not being catered for. We need more safe spaces and community hubs where people can go and train without worrying about how their needs may impact their experience.

One day recently, I checked my phone during a lunch break. That morning, I had received 295 text messages, more than 100 WhatsApp messages and who knows how many emails. On Instagram, TikTok and LinkedIn, I get about 800 messages on an average day. While I'm glad we're reaching more people, I can't help but feel guilty that there are so many people who need help, when it's physically impossible to get back to them all.

I've thought about this a lot. One way to try and support more people that has been suggested a lot is running virtual classes. In fairness, I loved what Joe Wicks did during the Covid lockdowns and I fully respect what he achieved. But I can't help thinking that his approach is more suited to fully able people.

So much of what I do is based on close personal relationships. The banter, and the eye contact and the jokes are as important as the exercise. It's all about the care and the love that I share with them, and there's no way to do that in an online class.

Also, as I said, people with disabilities have big variations in capabilities. If you have ten people with cerebral palsy, or Down syndrome, they'll all have different things they find easier or more challenging. When you're online, you obviously can't see the people you are training and what they can do. You're not there to help someone out of a chair, or sense if something is too much from their body language. And I don't ever, ever, ever want to upset anybody.

If I'm doing a Javeno's Online Workout, or whatever, and saying, 'OK, everybody wave your hands in the air!' – what about the people who can't do it? What about a Fran, trying to join in at home on her laptop, or an Aimee? I could easily be disrespecting people and making them

WHAT'S NEXT?

feel inferior. And that's the complete opposite of what we set up J7 to do. They might even – God forbid – get hurt.

So online classes might not be our future, but I still hope we can find a way to reach people all around the world. We receive global attention on social media, but my dream would be for us to physically train anyone who needs us. How can we do that? Well, I'm not sure I'm the right person to answer that question as I am a terrible businessman! I'm not joking! The other day, somebody asked me how many fee-paying members J7 has got. They were shocked when I told them that I don't know. Because I've never counted! And the reason I've never counted is because that's not the area I'm concerned with.

Most business owners will know all their numbers because they're so focused on making a profit and making money (understandably – we've all got bills to pay). To be honest, I never sit down and look at our numbers because . . . I can't be arsed. It's not where my interest lies so I have to let someone else manage that part. I'm not bothered. I'm very grateful that our fee-paying, able-bodied members choose to come to J7 over the other Manchester gyms they could join. But if they and *all* our members are happy, and we make enough to keep the centre running, I'm happy.

As long as my superstars, and all my ill, disabled and elderly clients, are having life-changing experiences within our orange walls, *that's* what I'm counting. *That's* the stuff that matters. And *that's* the bottom line at J7, not the bank balance.

But I do think about the future, about how many messages I am getting each day, and I do dream about how we can expand our mission. I'd like to open similar facilities around the world. I don't know how I'll do it yet but I want to make sure that, when I do, every gym is staffed with trainers who buy into what we've created in Manchester. Trainers who love the people they train.

I'd love a massive investor to come in and make it happen with me. Because that would be fantastic. But I'd never want to do our superstars, and our other clients, a disservice by getting the wrong people in. It would have to be an investor who shared our passion and our ideals. And, realistically, it may be hard to find that investor, because I wouldn't want a J7 anywhere in the world to be paid membership only. *I will never charge disabled people for training them.* We have to remain a facility that they can always go to for free. So any investor who comes in to help me take J7 global would have to be very, very big-hearted.

I can only do what I can. I'm only one person. I'll help anyone, and everyone, that I can . . . but I can't help the entire world. I can't please everyone. For now I'm at peace with that. I've not got much choice, really. But maybe in the future I'll find a way.

*

WHAT'S NEXT?

Somebody asked me, the other day, if I'm lucky enough to leave a legacy when I'm gone, what would it be? That's a very good question. And I've been thinking about my answer a lot.

I'd love my legacy to contribute to a world where disabled people don't feel like they're a burden or they're obstructing other people's lives. Not once in my life have I ever felt that anyone is a burden. If you care about someone, you don't think like that.

I'd like a world where parents teach their kids that if they see someone disabled, they don't bat an eyelid. A world where nobody does a double-take when they see a person with Down syndrome. Where kids don't look twice if they pass a double amputee in a wheelchair. They don't stop and stare. They just see another person.

My legacy would also be about enabling change. It would be empowering disabled people to have the confidence, and the voice, to speak up and say when something is wrong or unfair.

More than anything, I want to change society's attitudes towards disability. I want people to look at what we're doing and understand the real power of care. Because I genuinely feel as if I'm just getting started. There are a gazillion more DJs, Joshes, Aimees, Frans, Marleys, Shanias, Sophias, and Noahs out there for us to help.

This is all big picture stuff, I guess. I feel like I am someone who really lives in the present, which is maybe why I find it very hard to look into the future. Where will I be in ten years? Where will the superstars be in ten years? I just want the future to be a happy and healthy one. We'll never stop influencing people with goodness and positivity. And together, we'll never stop telling people: *you are not your limits.*

ACKNOWLEDGEMENTS

My big brother Tyrone, who always believed in me. Ty is the person who humbles me and he's a huge inspiration. He's cool, calm and the only person who can put me in my place if I am acting up. He tells me the brutal honest truth, as does my other brother, Trevor. Well, Trevor is actually my cousin but we're way closer than that. Trevor is my loudest support, and I cherish his advice more than anything because I know how much he loves me. He always tells me: 'Bet on yourself and you can't go wrong'. Ty and Trevor have my best interests at heart, and I look to them for guidance and reality checks.

My best friend, Ryan Worsley, has been by my side since we were 17 years old in college. He's never questioned my enthusiasm and has only ever encouraged it and supported me in the most powerful ways. Ryan always believed in me and the dream and vision for J7 that I created – even when it was only words on a piece of paper.

My family are my inspiration. Dwight, Shane, Trudy and Megan have always been my world, and I've only ever wanted to make them proud and improve their lives.

To anyone around the world who has liked, loved and supported my message, words and videos. To everybody who has shown interest in my life and allowed me to showcase my heart and true personality. To every single person who's ever walked through the doors at J7: I love and appreciate you all. To every single person around the world who has found motivation and happiness through my work: thank you for helping me positively change the world.

When I needed a manager, there was only one person I considered. My good friend for more than ten years: Hayley Thomas. Hayley, I thank you for all you do for me. The trust we have in each other is perfect. I'm grateful to have a friend who believes so much in me and my work. Thank you for investing so much in everything we do, and always making sure my integrity and principles are protected.

After one phone call, a magnificent lady called Carole Tonkinson instantly made me feel like this book had to happen. As my editor, she has been amazing, supportive and sincere. Thank you, Carole, for taking a chance on me. You are a beautiful soul and I believe we met for a reason.

ACKNOWLEDGEMENTS

Finally, I want to dedicate the book to my beautiful wife Laura, the love of my life, without you none of this would be possible, our two amazing sons, Mason and Leo, my unbelievable parents, Audrey and Clyde, and my two aunties, Aunty Norma and Aunty Adina. I'm only sad that Aunty Adina passed away before she got to see the success of J7 and the work we are doing.